Praise for *Virga & Bone*

"It's like Childs was born out of pink sandstone, given a mouth to speak, and has continued to defend his mother ever since. You'll read this book in one night but you'll reflect on it for a lifetime."
—ANNE HOLMAN, The King's English Bookshop

"Love songs earned in a life lived close to the wild."
—ALISON HAWTHORNE DEMING, author of
Zoologies: On Animals & the Human Spirit

"Craig Childs takes us not only through the external landscapes of the huge and wondrous; he takes us into and through himself."
—MARY SOJOURNER, author of *The Talker* and *29*

"A desert koan, Childs' latest is still and restive, full of unresolved pairings and brilliantly so. His 1,000-watt prose is as alive as the heat that makes the Mojave tick."
—ELIZABETH RUSH, author of
Rising: Dispatches from the New American Shore

"A tribute to the orphaned landscape of the borderlands."
—GREG CHILD, author of *Over the Edge*

"A bright hard gem of a book."
—WILL
A Great Ar

T0162929

VIRGA &BONE

ALSO BY CRAIG CHILDS

VIRGA & BONE

essays from dry places

CRAIG CHILDS

Illustrations by
Claire Taylor

TORREY HOUSE PRESS

SALT LAKE CITY • TORREY

First Torrey House Press Edition, October 2019
Copyright © 2019 by Craig Childs

Published by Torrey House Press
Salt Lake City, Utah
www.torreyhouse.org

International Standard Book Number: 978-1-948814-18-8
E-book ISBN: 978-1-948814-19-5
Library of Congress Control Number: 2019940780

Cover art "Bones of an Unknown Beast" by Claire Taylor
Interior art by Claire Taylor
Cover design by Kathleen Metcalf
Interior design by Rachel Davis
Distributed to the trade by Consortium Book Sales and
    Distribution

Torrey House Press offices in Salt Lake City sit on the homelands of Ute, Goshute, Shoshone, and Paiute nations. Offices in Torrey are in homelands of Paiute, Ute, and Navajo nations.

For the desert people,
wash-walkers and followers of desolation

CONTENTS

vərgə: *n.* rain that falls but evaporates
before touching ground

bōn: *n.* parts of the skeleton, what is left
when everything else erodes

INTRODUCTION

To write this book, I holed up on a far side of Tucson at the edge of the desert. In one direction the night was lit up, the city droned on, and in the other stood dark mountains, saguaros rising into stars. My writing table was up against a rammed earth wall in a modest cave of a house, no extra bedroom, no doors inside, a cistern shower in the bathroom and a composter for a toilet. I stacked and laid books on the work table, poetry mostly, Bass, Neruda, Oliver, Hoagland. There were a few longer reads, reminding me of what I was doing here: Abbey, Meloy, Lopez, Irvine. A mix of the living and the dead.

The place was empty but for a couch, a refrigerator, a wooden kitchen table, and a chair that I salvaged from a dumpster in the city. My friend next door, down a faint trail through cactus, offered the place for me to work. My gal saw a picture I texted and said it looked like I was writing in a Turkish prison, bare earthen floors and walls. She didn't see the sliding glass door I left open most of the day, and the clouds of spring-green creosote bushes and big-padded prickly pear cactus growing to the edge of worn steps. These weren't landscaping plants; they'd been growing here for centuries, swelling and shrinking with every rain and drought. Ribbed arms and heads of saguaros studded the skyline where Gila woodpeckers and curve-billed thrashers kept up conversation, and quail bobbed on the ground like sly, pear-sized hens. The Sonoran Desert in southern Arizona this time of year can be a circus. You have to get up sometimes and close the door to stay focused.

At night, my lamp on inside, pages rattled out of my keyboard. I looked up at a fox as it passed sleekly by, its nose almost touching the glass of the door slid closed. It glanced inside and trotted through creosote bushes where the dark of the desert took it back in.

A block away was the rest of Tucson, the desert crunched into lawns and landscape gravels. You could draw a line dividing here from there, light and darkness, mountains huddled back from the city and green from the rains and cool days of March, the other direction roofs.

I remember when I was a kid seeing road signs at the edge of Phoenix, after the last subdivisions, upon which people spray-painted SAVE OUR DESERT. Curve Ahead: SAVE OUR DESERT. Do Not Enter When Flooded: SAVE OUR DESERT. I hadn't put two and two together, I didn't know why the desert needed to be saved. Those places are gone now, stripped and replaced, little sense of what might have once been there. I don't know who did the graffiti in the 1970s, but when I was a kid, I imagined them dressed in bandanas, coming out of the desert, pushing against the city, defending forests of ironwood and saguaros, quail bursting into the air like little jets.

Driving back with groceries to the house where I was working, turning from pavement onto dirt, I stopped at a diamondback rattler half on and half off asphalt. It was drawing up warmth as the day ended, not a good idea with cars coming by. Did it know the dangers here, or was the snake not thinking *car, tires, weight, death?* I backed up until I could see along the length of its body from my rolled-down window. I told it to get off the road. It didn't. I opened the door, only got a head flinch, the snake laid out more or less straight, an arm and a half long with a mature stack of rattles at the end nearest me. Go, I said, waving my arms, and the rattler reluctantly moved. I got out and shooed it along as it picked up speed with a few half-hearted buzzes of its tail. As the head went into the base of a sprawling creosote, out of range of a strike, I took a notion to reach down and touch the rattle, let the thing buzz through my hand. How often does that happen? I could use a little snake medicine in this book, I thought. It was not something I'd ever done, but seemed doable. Following the slip of the tail, two inches away from grazing my fingers, I said, out loud, No.

What rattlesnake wants its rattle touched?

NO MOLESTAR LA FAUNA reads the sign outside of a biosphere reserve in the desert of northern Mexico, a few hours from here. The phrase rolls off the tongue. Don't molest the animals. Don't pick up desert turtles or pet rattlesnakes. The flora, while we're at it, needs no manhandling or groping, no more stately dead ironwoods stripped for campfires. We could save a planet obeying signs like these.

I kept thinking about that snake as I wrote during the night, its elegant scowl and the sinuous armor of its body, diamond-backed to blend with the shadows. It carries a neurotoxin that won't normally kill but will give you a run for your money, with swollen, coal-black appendages and hallucinations.

I've always been curious, but I'd rather not find out.

The snake is the desert. The fox is the desert, as is the bee that flew in through the open door while I was mincing words and attacked my head, stinging my face, shoulder, and scalp before I hurled it to the floor and squashed it, then staggered back to my keyboard. The country is not easy. Scorpions are here too, and a lush variety of cactus I would not touch, growing all around the house and in the arroyos up into the tapering ridges of the north Tucson Mountains. How could you not admire this sharpness? The buckled horizons and unencumbered views are nourishing. Poisonous things and needle-tip spines demand attention. A healthy agave with a fresh blade growing straight up, I never hesitate to reach out with a fingertip and touch, reminding myself every time how pointed they really are.

I go to the neighboring house a shouting distance away, a friend from way back. She has a painting on her wall by Pima-Maricopa artist Michael Chiago. It depicts an imagined ritual, could be any time in history, Native dancers coming out of the rainy desert down to the sea, barefoot and raising their hands and colorful tablitas to perform an ancestral rite. Waves wash onshore like glass. Lightning strikes in the distance through the purple smell of rain in the desert. I could stand at this painting for hours.

She brought me tequila in a glass with ice. A desert permaculturist by trade, it made sense she chose tequila, a spirit made from the heart of the agave. The flavor was bracing, stronger than I expected, including tinctures of medicinal desert herbs that she added. She said she made the tinctures herself, rendered from leaves and stems, said she always adds them to her tequila. I drank because it was good in an astringent way, because it tasted like rain and desert and the sting of alcohol. It tasted like where I am from.

All I think about sometimes is desert. Mountains or woods will do, but where I want to be at any given moment, if you catch me staring off, is where boulders are warm to the touch, where rain rarely falls and the air feels like it's being played on the highest, tightest string of a violin, as if you could barely squeeze a drop of water from it.

Some people dream in color. I dream in canyons. Shaded, echoing swirls; I will be flying, or floating rather, my shadow moving across the sandy floor. Maidenhair ferns grow from a blackened bedrock seep.

On the plains, with their rolling grasses and circular horizons, I look for bare patches, prairie dog towns and lonely buttes. I imagine if it were drier, what it could look like someday, salt flats, hexagonal buckles frosted with halite, not a bush or an ant to be seen. When it's pure desert, nothing but drought, you see the bones of the world. You see what it's all made of. I'm not saying it's better this way or that I want the world to turn to desert. I'm just a fan.

I traveled to Tibet for a month on assignment and on the long flight to Beijing I sat in steerage rows thinking, *Utah*. What I could do with a month in Utah.

Some are born to it. Some come to it later, not realizing until the skyline breaks a certain way and banners of virga fall from clouds toward the desert floor, but don't quite touch, that they had come home. You've chewed on green twigs of Mormon tea, pulping ephedrine out of them to the cadence of rock underfoot and the hush of wash sand, walking the dry runnels of southern Arizona or northern Mexico, or the red arroyos of the Four Corners. If you're going to be in the desert, I recommend encountering it in all of its forms. Rain, rock, dry, sand, canyon, mesa, beach. Take it into yourself. If you don't think the water you've found is good, take only a sip, or touch it from your fingertips to your lips. If it doesn't taste like salt, and it's old rainwater in a bedrock depression, even if there are a few swollen berries of bighorn droppings on the bottom, or, if it's a big tank, a dead bat is floating at the surface, it's probably okay to drink. It will keep you alive.

Yes, I've had giardia.

This book is about pieces of the desert, its elements, its waters and winds. These pages are odes to what I see as ingredients making up the arid Southwest, the parts you take inside yourself one at a time, or sometimes all at once.

I've chosen not to name characters because this is not about people. It is about essence. People are present only for scale. Some stories were easy to tell, flowing without looking up, and others I crumpled over, could hardly make sense of what happened. Any story should be this way. It should feel like pulling something burning out of yourself. There you find what you are devoted to.

Mostly I wrote inside, so I didn't wander off. I left the house as few times as possible, going as far as climbing a metal ladder propped against a ramada out the back door. I sat on the corrugated roof and looked across boulder flanks of chocolate-colored mountains. My friend living next door has protected this land for decades, making a pariah of herself to county planners for being a watchdog, for not letting million-dollar homes go up on this patch of desert, for fighting roads and pavement and the wells drying up or turning to poison, and not growing rich over her labors, using rainwater catchment, turning waste into soil, one of the most noble ways I know of living. To have a ramada in the desert and rainwater in the cistern is enough. To have time to sit and take it in is double the blessing. From the roof I took advantage of this blessing and watched saguaros do nothing, all of them silent as if waiting for one in the group to speak. A notebook was open on my lap and I began to write about the sea.

Tucson Mountains, Arizona
Bean Tree Farm
March 2019

VIRGA

If I could see the wind, it would look orchestral: strands and swirls nested into each other, braiding and springing apart. When it stills and coolness settles, the air would lie as smooth as water on a lake.

Flying over the Four Corners in August, we couldn't see the wind, but we could feel it. We were riding inside an aluminum box with wings, the heat-pan of the desert boiling below. It was good flying until about one in the afternoon, which was now, as a big up carried us through the hoop of a thermal and down the other side.

Time to be on the ground, said the pilot, turning us west toward the blue snakes of Lake Powell. He had a few years of experience with planes, a good and trusted friend from the backcountry, a novice growing less novice with every trip. It was only the two of us, crammed more tightly than astronauts in a space capsule. We knew the drill, talking about landforms through our headsets, memorizing canyons and redrock swales, making maps in our heads. We had gear to go on foot from wherever we landed, checking dirt strips around the Nokai Dome, not far into Utah from the Arizona desert. Clouds were scattered and some bloomed into cumulus risers, a pattern of the day, heat lifting from blush-colored earth, entering higher, cooler air, condensing to moisture that sometimes, when everything is right and the prayers have been said and a feather from the wing of a hawk sails up on a thermal, dew drops gathering on its edges at twenty thousand feet, condensing as moisture that falls as rain.

No rain today. Clouds had a whiteness that said don't even think about it.

Hall's Crossing, he said. See it out there? He handed me the map and his finger scooted down to the electronic screen on his knee, checking distances. We both preferred dirt, but this landing strip was paved and it was close and safe. That's a reason I fly with him. He's cautious. He caught a whiff of something the other day, passing at sunrise in front of the Bears Ears buttes in southern Utah, and he turned the plane around without hesitation, didn't say anything until we'd pulled a complete, gentle U-turn. As he scanned the terrain ahead, calculating a possible landing at Monticello, Blanding, or Bluff, envisioning his approach in case of power loss or disabled flaps, he asked, Do you smell something? I detected nothing but the slightly musty smell of a machine and old upholstery, a mix of body shop and furniture repair. He asked again. A burning smell or chemical? I said no. We flew on until he was convinced it was nothing and turned us back on our route. He didn't have to explain why he'd been concerned. Up here, small mistakes add up quickly.

The pilot and I fly together whenever we can. A couple years back we explored not far north of here, bringing backpacks and hopping one rutted old mining strip to the next in the Utah desert. That had been in October in mostly gentle air, cool days and crisp nights, perfect for flying. August is different. Days are planned around temperature, airborne at the first crack of light, the coolest part of the day, and back on the ground by one, two at the latest, before the sky turns into an inferno of upward winds. The plane needs lift, something to fly on. Hot air is thinner, fewer molecules to push against, not a solid hold. An old cloth-wing like this, a 1946 vintage, needs good lift to stay airborne and resist the punishing updrafts and downdrafts of a shimmering desert afternoon.

Hall's Crossing was the closest landing between slim canyons written in cursive, the airstrip sitting alone on a plain of rock and sand that goes on for miles, for days, forever. We landed, hiked around the area, cooked dinner, and settled in. Just after sunset, I walked the blacktop back and forth, talking on the phone with my kids. The pilot was at his tent, sitting outside with a screen in his face, studying the weather maps, his plane tied down and blocked. Love and giggles on the phone, and a voice deepening, asking what I was doing. A few days out by plane, I said, having a look at the desert, leaving at the start of light to see where the day pushes us.

Hard conversations sometimes, questions from home, a girl, a school grade, a thing said or done. I lay on my back on the hot runway. Air temperature tonight would barely dip below ninety degrees. Nothing was cool, definitely not the runway. Knees crooked upward, my spine settled on an oven-top, back of my skull on asphalt, I talked through whatever hard thing it was, searching for words, giving sketchy advice at best, letting the runway cook me from below. We exchanged goodnights and I love yous. Phone off, the evening sky returned, stars not out yet. I sat up from the runway and looked across a horizon of distant scarps, redrock turned black. Some of the clouds in the west, backlit by an indigo dusk, were letting out spiderwebs of virga, rain falling in long and gossamer veils, but not touching ground.

You wait in heat like this, scanning the horizon for a cloud, sometimes through a haze of wildfire smoke that turns the world orange, when a drop of rain would be a miracle. You stop in the middle of the day and hold up your hand to the sky, the mountains on the horizon electrified. If the air had more water, if it were East Coast on a sharp summer day, the sky would be washed out and white, hard to tell distances until a plane flies through. In dry like this, you can see into the blue lens of space, eye set to infinity.

When you hear the word *drought* in the desert, it means magnification. These dry, rocky places are made of drought, created by absence, the sky holding back on purpose. When a drought is in drought, a knob with very fine settings is being turned, every hundredth of a degree boiling harder. I saw a creek by my house, which I'd always seen running, dry up and not start again for a year, beaver having trundled off to who knows where, or died in their dens waiting for moisture from the sky.

Deserts are mummifiers, bone-makers. Some years, the rain won't come, clouds promising and promising, but did you say the right prayers, did you pray to the right god? Global measurements

of desert precipitation had to be recalibrated recently when it was discovered that satellite signals
were bouncing off of virga and not actual rain.
Fifty percent of estimated rainfall never reached
the ground.

By morning, virga was gone, horizons played
out and cloudless. Loaded before dawn in the
earliest light, headlamps in the cockpit, the pilot showed me his screen and the day's coming
weather. I asked about the green blob down by
the town of Kayenta, the tail end of Comb Ridge,
northern Arizona. A little thunderstorm, he said.
It was left over from yesterday, not much to it. I
asked if we could aim for that, at least get a look
at the only thing happening in a hundred miles.
He agreed.

Takeoff was slow, the ascent lagging on, night
temps not low enough to cool the surface. We
would have picked another week, but you take the
one you planned, the hottest August on record, air
thin and rising.

No pilot likes spending too much time near
the ground. You don't have space to improvise
a few hundred feet up, where the ground could
rise up in seconds. We both leaned into the climb,
our shoulders forward, as if giving the engine that
much more weight. After five miles we leveled off
at two thousand feet, air propping us up better,
high enough to relax. Once you're up, the world

is yours, seventy to eighty knots, like driving through the sky with a tractor.

Around nine we landed at Goulding's Trading Post on the Monument Valley end of the Navajo Nation. We tied down and crossed a paved road for milkshakes at the gas station, weaving between RVs and tour trucks with open-air beds, the morning crowd already rolling, an hour and a half away from a hundred degrees. We took on extra fuel and chatted with a retired German couple who'd landed in a silver-tipped single prop with chrome exhaust ports. They were out to see the sights of the Southwest from the air. Their plane cruised five thousand feet above our altitude at a couple hundred knots. They raved, as much as a retired German couple raves, about flying in the West. They said Europe is like a traffic jam, radios crackling nonstop with flights in every direction, landings and turns, every decision announced, airspace chopped up over cities and towns. Out here, they said, you could do anything, be any-where. You'd go half an hour without hearing a stranger's voice through your headset.

The benefit of our plane was that it flies low and slow, more often under the clouds than over. Going through his checklist, the pilot tapped his screen where the green blob from dawn had moved north over Monument Valley. This is our last up today, he said. When we land, that's where we're staying. Where do you want to go?

I pointed to the blob of weather. Usually we flew in accordance to landscape, aiming for buttes, pivoting around mountains. We'd check on airstrips or scan for routes we could later take on foot, seeing if water holes had any water. The air has equal terrain, invisible canyons and vast, open bays to fly through and around.

Since he'd gotten his license a few years earlier, I'd watched the pilot test himself between the topography of earth and sky. He's not a bumbling risk-taker, but he pushes his boundaries. It's the only way to keep flying. If you don't learn, he said, you aren't going anywhere. If the first landing didn't work, bouncing across a trough plowed by a tractor in the 1950s on the cap of a southern Utah mesa, repaired only a few times since then, he'd swing back for a second attempt, and a third, until he figured out how his plane works, how it responds to ruts, bouncing and throwing gravel, struts creaking, and he'd stick it on the fourth try.

The green on his screen had no yellow or red, no alarming colors. It was a smear of low pressure, a memory of a storm from the night before. If he thought it was dangerous, he would have kept us away. Approaching from the north at four thousand feet, about seventy knots, we saw an unremarkable cloud, a vestige of a cumulonimbus, a thunderhead on its last breath. Beneath it fell a single drape of virga. The cloud was letting go of itself, disgorging strands of spider's silk that tumbled toward the towers of Monument Valley, stone Yeibichai dancing into a desert basin. At an altitude of about a thousand feet, the heat of the desert was too much, the dew point too low to let the rain make it all the way. On the ground beneath it, I'd be standing on peach-red sand, boulders shimmering all around, my hands open to the sky, and I'd be looking straight up asking for nothing.

The Navajo word for water is *tó*, pronounced *twuh*, the word shortened at the end, the sound of a drop of water landing. Virga is a Navajo koan, the sound of one drop not landing, waterless for those down below. My word for water sounds like *want*, sounds like *desire*, which might not be so different from the Navajo. Can we fly through it? I asked. The pilot looked over at the sheen of drizzle, a single curtain. He judged distances and potential turbulence in air that had been stable since we left the trading post half an hour earlier. He said we should find out and tipped the plane, her wings shading us from the sun as we arced toward this floating steamship and its diaphanous trailer.

Entering the virga was not as rough as we thought it would be. Expecting rattles and jolts, we instead sank into a well, our stomachs rising as we dropped. He increased power and lifted us back up. We could see raindrops: lone, silver-gray beads streaking by. They hit the wings and passed my window where I watched them fall, trailing several hundred feet before hissing back into air.

One drop hit the rounded windscreen, then another, a fifth, an eleventh. They were soft as cooked peas, as ripe berries. Each became a small, staggering comet heading around the plexiglass, looking for a way off, a way down, wanting nothing more than to meet the ground.

The plane fell again as we crossed the virga's middle, then fell once more, riding down a staircase, the veneered cloth wings catching us as the pilot throttled back up. Cooler air descended inside the falls, carried down by water droplets, causing the air to sink. Only a few more drops fell against the windscreen as we tilted out the other side. It was five seconds across, a tenth of a mile thick.

Virga, I can now say, is as velveteen as it looks. This was no downpour, technically a drizzle. I could have stood inside its rain and barely gotten wet.

Out from under the cloud's shadow, we became a shadow on the ground ourselves, a dot passing over sand dunes and open-mouthed arroyos. Our shadow was a storyteller crossing buttes and billows of rocks the size of small towns. In a canyon full of shadows, our plane winked out the daylight, a flash across a damp clutch of maidenhair ferns and a small pillow of moss where water seeps through a seam in the rock, a tiny spring releasing ancient rainwater.

SPRINGS

I stood on a breezy flank of the Panamint Dunes in Death Valley National Park, looking around the barren horseshoe mountain range that allowed these dunes to exist. I had no idea where one could find water. With the highest temperatures in North America and some of the lowest rainfall, the Mojave Desert is bare and sharp, almost nothing but rock. If not rock, sand. Where would you start?

I thought of myself as a water hunter. Trained in desolate places, I looked for rain holes, springs, seeps. I learned to follow bees and trace geologic layers, keeping note of the taste of water from one canyon to another, hunting through halls of sandstone for a clutch of moss and fern emerging from a crack. I picked up simple techniques, digging in sandy washes to find stores of moisture, seeing underground with imaginary X-ray eyes where buried bowls in the bedrock held water under the sand. I waited for nightfall and the water table to rise, dampness around cottonwood roots lifting with it. I've hung plastic over plants and collected very little to drink by morning, and boiled seawater in a pressure cooker to make it barely potable.

First time in Death Valley felt like I was starting over. I could make out the green cluster of a small spring town, a relative oasis, about fifteen miles down from the dunes in a pale, wind-struck, flat-bottomed valley. But that's not what I was after. Trees in the settlement were imported, the ice cream at the gas station expensive. I was thinking of water if I needed it, how it might make itself known in these reared-back mountains lifting a few thousand feet, earth monsters barren of nearly all vegetation. Snow had fallen up high, leaving taller mountains downrange white-stroked. It would melt and fill the insides of mountains, most going into aquifers and subterranean rivers flowing unseen from one basin to the next. A desert spring researcher out of Northern Arizona University told me that little springs were all over the place in this valley. The researcher was heading out to document springs on the nearby military grounds of China Lake, California, and he waved his hand in the air as if gesturing across all of the Mojave Desert. Springs were all over the place, he said.

In this ring of peaks, a city of dunes rising from the back end, I saw nothing that might resemble water, not the kind you could take in your mouth and drink.

I guided years ago in Anza-Borrego, in the Mojave east of San Diego, lost a client through a palm oasis where she got away from me, climbing and scrabbling upward, maybe on drugs. Or maybe the smell and sound of water pouring over rock, the skirted shade of palm trees and the brittle aridity everywhere, got to her. I spotted her way ahead running like a monkey up the canyon, heading for the source, which I'd already told her not to, not with me guiding. I sent the rest back to camp and followed her for about an hour up through uneasy boulder fields and rock-jumps over water. She was a city dweller, strong and smart enough, but she was making leaps I thought twice about, smeared with fresh mud from her hand, her shoes soaked and leaving a pattern on rock. I found her coming back down through a brushy declivity with mud on her face, and a grin that made me forget how damn worried I was, the paperwork and the search and rescue contingencies. She was breathless. She didn't need any help at all. I told her she'd worried the shit out of me and please don't do that again, but did you find the source? She smiled, as if she'd found something impossible, and nodded yes.

Water does something to you. It's like finding gold, but more shimmer, less money. It is the purer element.

Standing on the dunes, I didn't need palm trees and sparkling, dancing water. Just a drip would do, a spot of moss, a dribbling grotto. It should be marked, I thought, not with a sign screwed into rock, but by cattails, watercress, maidenhairs . . . I didn't know what grew out here. I was a stranger. Even with binoculars every rocky face and canyon looked the same.

Coming up the swell of a dune, my gal was carrying a day pack, walking barefoot. We were out on a date in the desert. We'd been courting for a few years and we walked easily together, our feet warm in the sand.

The Panamint Dunes are egg whites whipped up into peaks at the head of Panamint Valley, a pearl seated in a thuggish pendant. Everything around the dunes is either pan or broken, staggering rock and mountain, the ground pebbled and bouldered, not a place you'd want to walk barefoot. Rocks that look like shark teeth and hatchets stick up from the ground, or they splinter into books. Anything that grows means soil poisoned by fallen leaves, or spiny urchins prying between rocks, or sandpaper leaves on bushes that look like they're from Mars. Again, not barefoot.

On the dunes, nothing grew. Nothing was sharp. We left tracks around the last few boulders, pieces of gray dolomite sanded smooth like small whales breaking the surface.

The sky behind us ripped like thunder. We both turned to see a fighter jet blazing along the edge of the dunes at eye level. My partner pumped her arm in the air, like getting a trucker to pull the horn. The pilot saw the gesture, a helmet turning for a half a second. In response, the throttle opened up, wings snapped in a fuel-burning greeting, a wave hello back to her. The jet punched forward in a dazzling roar, tipping into a U-turn at the amphitheater toe of the Panamint Mountains.

Aerial flight training and combat are regular features of Death Valley. You shield your eyes from the sun, searching for the source of a tight-throated roar overhead, the planes moving well in front of their sound. I don't get mad at this sort of crap. Blowing a hundred thousand dollars to race a sleek, sound-barrier-breaking projectile with a joystick between your legs, navigating an ancient and fallen realm bare to the bone—not some virtual nonsense but the actual sky—even I'd consider a little of that. It's the wars I don't like.

I stood on the dune slope awed by the sheer power of what I saw. I suspected the pilot was showing off, giving a show for us mortals on the ground. As the jet banked hard, two blue circles of flame made eye contact with us. The pilot pushed back down the valley, laying it out in the opposite direction, still at eye level, and we were the cheerleaders, pompoms pumping in the air.

Combat air space is a desert element, no trees to block out what you're seeing, few or no towns to disturb the dark. Sitting up at night at a small, darkened camp, you watch dogfights from two thousand feet off the deck up to the stratosphere, red lights looping and diving, engines straining like thunder escaping through pinholes. Do you admire all those wires and plates and hours of g-force training, drill rigs plumbing the earth? What went into making a person be able to dive and swerve like a hawk? It's hard not to accidentally admire power and grace, at the cost of so many wars. That's what you see from the desert.

The mountains where I saw the most aerial action were at the bottom end of the Basin and Range from Arizona into Mexico, bare and darkened, metamorphic rocks and volcanics scratching the sky, broad valleys between. Saguaros stand across the sloped bajadas, days-long floors threaded with ironwood tree washes, flash flood debris bungled in bushes of ragweed and acacia. This is how you find water. Follow the lifelines up. Sometimes there'd be a spring, sometimes a tank, a tinaja, a rainwater hole drilled in the rock.

In Death Valley, I saw no slightly verdant washes, no green bands of thornscrub surrounded by spiny Joshua trees. I could see life out there, but not much of it: sparse coverage of creosote, like ghost shadows fanned across the rocky apron of the dunes. There were waves of nothing but rock, ramp lands, far-off highway invisible but for the odd, bullet-like car sweeping across the wasteland. The oasis town was specks of buildings glinting in the sun around a cluster of palms and voluptuous, salty tamarisk trees. No trees in the rest of the desert, nothing green from several thousand feet in elevation down to the stark pan of sea level in this ocean-less Mojave.

A wildlife refuge had allowed me permission to measure and map water holes near the border with Mexico in southwest Arizona. In the serrated mountains of Cabeza Prieta I taught myself how to find natural tinajas filled with enough old rain to carry and drink. I used old maps and a Jesuit's journal to find some of the holes, dark wells in solid rock. My search for water was focused, my life depending on it. Death Valley offered its water to me differently, not through focus but serendipity.

This would be the year of wildflowers, a super bloom. Most of Death Valley's backroads were closed due to late winter flooding, and the snow line was heavy down to eight thousand feet or so. Our days were clear with the crispness of late winter, mare's tails high and feathered. We'd arrived days after more precipitation than the park had received in years. Looking at the place, you wouldn't know such a bloom was beginning, the land the color of late-summer grass not watered for months, broken up by charcoals and undersea grays. Close your eyes and think geology. That is the color of Death Valley. Talc mines, borax mines, chloride, salt, gypsum. Think of any mineral power and it's probably been mined here.

That night at camp, where we'd carried packs into a small bay of sharply weathered dolomite, we had a sip of whiskey and set over the map with headlamps, moving through contours, pausing up in the wells of canyons where geology was piled all over itself. Springs were marked on the map, blue squiggles dangled from blue circles, like a symbol for an organism, a fusion of geology and water. Marked springs were isolated in the vaults of mountains, not down on the massive debris fans below. I imagined them dripping out of rock. Tomorrow we'd try some of these canyons, see where they go, find any water they might hold. We shut off our lights and looked up at red lights swooping, pinhole roars trailing behind, signs of desert and wars far away, and a full moon turning the night into a dream.

I will be a doddering old man looking for water, pausing in someone's backyard in Bermuda shorts and loafers, on my hands and knees to drink out of the sprinkler as my kids or orderlies run over to stop me. I'll be the grump in the window waiting for rain.

The last thing my brain ever thinks might be *water*, the taste of it, too much of it, and too little. On my headstone, inscribe the sign of a spring.

The place you inhabit gets into you, the minerals you eat and breathe, the way the sky is shaped in your eye. I prefer the dry places. Strong horizons, sometimes cloud-streaked with virga, sometimes sheeted with rain, usually empty, the ground most of the time open-mouthed and thirsty, not a drop for most of the months of the year.

I found a spring coming out near an ancestral site in Arizona, a place where water flowed through rock and a nest of roots. It was not far from an ancient cliff dwelling just off an interstate. I peeked into the roots and clear-flowing water coming out at gallons per minute, and saw a paho, a painted prayer stick, likely Hopi, a marker, an offering, a feather or two hanging from it. This was a spring people had known for a long time, probably by clan, a map of a culture, a map of water. It is an offering you would not touch.

The water, though, put that to your lips. It might not be good advice, but in the desert you should almost always drink the water. I cupped my hand in that spring and drank and it tasted like a cave.

I drank what I found in Death Valley. It was easy with rains just days before. I sipped out of a break in a boulder, a hole the shape of a prism, the shape of crystalline pink rhyolite. It tasted clean, at least as clean as the sky. If my senses were keener, I might be able to taste the parts per million of jet fuel and wayward urban exhaust, a tang of acid from molecular breakdown, or the base note of elevating carbon. It's never just rain, never clean water from the sky. It doesn't have the dissolved pharmaceuticals and birth control pills of most tap water, depressants and antidepressants able to flow through treatment plants and sold in plastic bottles made entirely of post-consumer karma. What it does have is an infusion of molecules that rise above every city and industry.

If I knew this water well enough, I could name the storm it came from, its journey across the Pacific, the islands and mainlands that its wave of air had touched. *Clean* is all I came up with. Clean because it didn't come through a pipe or through stacks of metal screens, but from the sky.

These little boulder pools aren't springs. They have no mechanical parts, as the word implies. Springs are made of pressures and gradients. They are controlled by coarseness of rock grains deep underground, angles of bedding in the formation. Capillary action that goes on for miles, pulling water through a geologic filtration process, sky-lighting wherever the earth will allow.

In other deserts, I'd find a cottonwood tree marking water, stately gray trunk with high, fluttering leaves, and a softness in the gravel, water emerging from a dark and shiny seam. In the back of a canyon in Death Valley, nothing. Iron-orange, iron-red, gray like old silverware, the rock back here was the meat of the planet. You can tell water flows because the rocks move, transported by countless tons out of the mountains, through these canyons, into winding, shallow arroyos that spread across enormous fans reminding one of the oversized scale of Martian landscapes, as if you were marching along a debris fan off Olympus Mons.

As we crossed a fan miles wide—not a tree, not a reference, little sense of small or large or far away—I looked ahead and she'd disappeared, her gait faster than mine. Check that, she was there, but she'd become a piece of geology, a bit of color in motion against ragged chocolates and grippy, gray boulders. When she found a new color, she called it out and waited for me, announcing, We got pinks! Or placing a rock in my hand, saying it reminds her of coral. Another she picked up was like a sherd of broken, painted pottery, which she called Mojave black-on-red. She was making up her own desert dictionary, she said. Instead of using proper nomenclature, she named rock pebblecrap and bric-a-brac, because if you're not thinking of water out here, you're thinking of rock.

We got up into a narrow, winding canyon, foot of the mountains, rocks upon boulders upon rocks, debris flows and geologic dumps, our voices muffled turn by turn. She asked if this place were a graveyard for rocks, or if this was their rave room, their jungle lounge, geology having the time of its life.

Where would water come out of this mess of taffied metamorphic, this pebblecrap, how would it find a way through? This wasn't too pressing a question, one of many when you're in a new place, but I kept my eye out for a brow of monkey flowers or ferns. It continued to be all rock. We went up one canyon after the next, hard to tell which went deepest into the mountains because some cliffed out, leaving us at dead, boxy ends, while others that seemed large at the mouth skinnied into pinches and rockslides, not much of canyons at all, and all of them dry.

* * *

That night we camped like Philistines off the highway in a gravel turnaround with eleven other vehicles. A man who said he was from San Francisco made the rounds with a case of Coors Light, handing a can to anybody who wanted one. My gal and I set up folding chairs out the backside of an Outback with Colorado plates, watching the sun set across Death Valley proper, light coming through breaks in low, spindrift clouds. There'd be precipitation tonight. The last month in Death Valley had more rainy than sunny days, saved by the bell after a prolonged drought that would likely start up again as suddenly as it seemed to stop. Deserts do that. Especially deserts in a time of dangerously tremulous climate fluctuations around the world, a tradeoff for jets racing up and down the valleys and expensive ice cream at a tamarisk oasis along the highway.

That night it rained only a short while, then a liberal few inches of snow fell. All night, the tent walls slid and shushed. By first light, we woke to full coverage, every creosote bush a white plume drooping to the ground, which was itself covered, not a gap to be seen. The air did not move, not a drift or cornice. In the yawn of Death Valley, snow level was down to a thousand feet. The barren country below, down to sea level and lower, was rained on but not white like the desert a thousand feet higher. A raven was the only dark thing, flying in for snowcapped picnic tables on its daily rounds, landing breast deep, wings up in the air to balance itself in this unfamiliar substrate.

A trucker came through on the highway, pulled over after a harrowing mountain pass behind him. In thirty-some years of driving this route, he said, he'd never seen it like this. It was like trying to get over the high Sierra in a February blizzard, his tracks cutting fresh, unplowed snow. Maybe he stopped because we should know. With license plates from all over, most of us didn't know what planet we were on, least of all the little girl just above toddler age who was camped with her dad, romping around from one car to the next and throwing snow into the air. The truck driver said this was a once in a lifetime thing to see. He climbed in and drove on, his big tires slopping through the slush toward lower elevations where the canyons we'd walked the day before had flooded, the highway across Death Valley mudded and graveled.

Asking around the campground, I came up with a mean temperature of thirty degrees. The ground felt five or ten degrees warmer, as ground tends to. The snow had started to melt as soon as it touched down. Water was born. Not something I had to hunt for, it came to me. It was already beginning to darken and pool with the sun obscured behind a scrim of clouds. When the sun broke out, blinding against solid-white mountains, the melt quickened, threads of parking lot mud stretching like piano wire into the desert where they sank as if they had to keep falling. Water needed to go deeper.

Salt soaked it up in no time. A couple hundred feet below sea level where it had rained all night and didn't snow, salt flats were by afternoon dry and firm. Brushing a fingertip over the ground, the roughness was like a slightly mineralized feather, no moisture detected.

In the salt, which occupies a fair portion of Death Valley, enough that it rivals mountains for geographic dominance, precipitation goes under when it lands, as if stepping on a trap door, falling into a transient water table that floats beneath the surface within a nearly solid matrix of salt. That's the top of basin-floor hydrology.

The aquifers of Death Valley, and all of its surrounding valleys, are within a gauntlet of giant fault blocks, where groundwater getting out would be like swimming through crowded icebergs. What falls in Death Valley, and gets underground, stays in Death Valley, making it, ironically, a reservoir. Because it is the lowest point on the land, water flows downhill into it, sinking beneath the surface, waiting.

We were on the pool cover, the thin skim of salt. Walking out with a hundred others felt like an inexplicable family reunion, people who shouldn't know each other, but somehow do, meandering through one another, families and couples, and people on their own, no sign pointing where to go, no reason to be in one place or another. We were on the salt flats, ground made entirely of salt-ridged polygons, each big enough you could curl up inside its borders. Children ran, some in flat-out sprints, playing their bodies across what felt like a limitless expanse. Mountain ranges lay to either side and in the middle, on a snow-white pan that extended for miles, languages passing in and out of each other. We drifted between parties, pretending to talk to each other while we listened in, picking out Russian, Vietnamese, German, French, English. We'd try to guess ahead and were usually wrong.

Out past the people and their fanciful assemblage, she and I walked across hoar-frosted salts, a polychromatic white as if looking across the edge of a prism. No one else was ahead of us. Why walk out this far when every five feet is the same? We had nowhere to go, growing smaller on the horizon, stopping to sit on the flatness where she got on her knees, dipped her head, and took a very small nip of salt in her mouth, testing it first, then saying it tasted like it was from a salt shaker.

More than half a mile onto the flat, we were the only two stabs of life. We came into a slightly lower part of the pan. The salt was softening, becoming a little mushy. Skimming a finger across it, I found moisture in the graying grains. We'd entered the water table, not standing water, but absorbed into the surface. Soon, there was a small hole, a fracture in the salt, and it held clear water. She recoiled, and then stared, as I scooped some up in my fingers and put it in my mouth. This was the bottom of the surface-geology, the place all the softest minerals went, suspended in a deceptively clear fluid. The cells in my mouth constricted. I could barely swallow, not enough to make me sick, but enough it burned down my throat. It tasted more like seawater, I said, than seawater. Without the presence of fish, without seaweed or an octopus, the water was devoid of any taste of life, just earth, the powdery, astringent part of earth. I offered her some and she declined.

At dusk, a stillness gathered, like one just before you remember what you were looking for, like before the sneeze. We took off through side canyons near where we'd carried our packs for the night, exploring our surroundings. It was all water, but none that stood or flowed, none you could put your finger on. The shape was water, geology and hydrology. We walked these canyons into the dark, their cemented substrate of rocky flood debris carved open, wound around itself like a spiral. A squiggle on the map, it was a place where water had been, where two nights ago it flowed strong in the rain and now was dry.

After midnight, wind came on hard. The gusting back end of last night's storm howled through a small side canyon where we camped. Skies stayed clear. Any rainwater or snowmelt that collected on the rock was now peeled away. Sleep was fitful and buffeted, tent walls taking big breaths before deflating across our faces. Any water had to go under to survive.

Mountains are lakes. Their bellies hold rainfall and snowmelt. Their inner cracks and wells of conglomerates or sedimentary rock act as banks. There are always leaks, loose plates, broken plumbing. There are always springs.

On the map, we picked a spring where Death Valley runs into the Ibex Wilderness. It was marked on the side of a mountain, in one of a few nameless canyons, couldn't tell which.

In the wettest winter in years, the whole of the land still appeared to be swallowed in drought, a sight pleasing to my eye, to every sense of mine. If the place had trees, rolling horizons of pine tops, it still would have been beautiful, but without the sharper elements of desolation, starkness, mineral, tectonics, erosions. A pine forest is missing a layer the desert reveals.

We moved up wide-open, blown-out canyons of pink, pebbled volcanics, and rocks colored in blues, purples, browns. She was ahead of me and shouted, *Water!* Then shouted more water. She hopped up the drainage and I could scarcely keep up with her. No palms or promenades of trees, this spring came out from under rocks and barely changed the space around it. A little more grass, a little greener, but I wouldn't have spotted this from far off. Waving her arms from a boulder top, she said it kept going, water upon water. I wouldn't call it a stream. It was more like water taking a breath and then holding it in, filling rock pools enough to trickle one to the next. Where it flowed across polished bedrock, the water was sheathed in morning ice, gulping and squiggling just beneath a half-clear surface.

This spring wasn't a baptismal font, not a fountain, a faucet, or even a place where I could stop to say this is it, leave your offerings here. Water vanished for fifty or a hundred feet, and we picked it up again, finding it at contact points between geologic formations, and places where sand had been swept out by storms, where envelopes opened in the ground, gathering moss and ice. The source was a perforation in the earth that drew my mind underground, seeing through

labyrinths and stony blockages, rain from ice ages
and everything after adding what it could, no well
to take this up, no creaky windmill filling a tank. I
tasted it, and it was clean.

Wiry and quick, she continued hopping up
the canyon, bounding from rock to rock, almost
out of shouting distance. I kept hearing her saying
water, laughing out loud, gasps of giddy excite-
ment as she climbed up this small, untroubled
spring, disappearing for a moment, then exposed
against the sky above me.

EXPOSURE

It was a standoff, a dark truck every half mile or so aimed our direction, and in the middle, the searing roar of Burning Man. We'd walked for six days through the Black Rock Desert to get this far, a few miles from the thrumming city and its bursts of flame striking a clear, blue sky.

On the playa, an Ice Age lake bed, once the largest freshwater lake in North America and now a giant pale mirror, nothing stood or grew off the ground. From the trucks' points of view, the only thing out here was us, not a drop of water but for what we carried.

We had tickets to get in, so we figured there wouldn't be a problem—we'd hop the fence and walk into the middle of this monstrosity of sound and sculpture. There'd be no hopping. We were the tallest things out here, besides the circus-like metropolis of Burning Man, its structures shimmering in morning heat. One of the trucks started up and rooster-tailed to us. It was a beaten-up road truck with alligator treads on the tires. Guy inside, nose-boned and bearded, told us we had to stop our course and circle around the city to the entrance. We gathered at his window, pulling out a BLM map and pointing to our location, explaining we were still outside the private-use exclusionary boundary. He looked at our map and was quiet for a moment. He said we had half a mile and needed to start veering off.

I originally had a picture of us coming in as shambling travelers blending in with the desert. We'd be stealthy hobgoblins and we'd move closer by night, then in the morning walk straight ahead like we knew what we were doing.

Reality: you can't do anything out here without someone seeing.

I shouldn't be here, I should never have come. Northern Arizona, we got dropped off on a Navajo reservation backroad and walked in from there. In hindsight, not a great idea for two rambling, bearded white guys with packs almost the size of coffins. You don't do a thing out here without someone spotting you. That's what I forgot.

The plan was to meet anyone along the way, come calling at a hogan offering pomegranates or whatever we had, back before I learned you were supposed to bring Bluebird Flour and good coffee. I was younger, then. I didn't believe in borders. The land I saw was not about humans, but about terrain and the direction of rivers. The only hogan we found was wind-splintered, its beams fallen into silver hulks, an open mouth on the ground that was once a living space. We did not step inside the ruin.

A canyon took us in, shadows nervously plumbing down to where old Douglas fir grew and snow crusted the ground. Springs along the floor were wrapped in ice. Mountain lion tracks, the revered puma, were all over, fresh as a day or two. It appeared to be hunting, on the move, checking its stations over and over. On the third day we saw human tracks, three people, not sure who they were, but at this point it was best to find the shortest distance out and not meet anyone, a few more days at most.

We walked and climbed through museums of archaeology, places where one ought not to be. We felt in our bones too much broken pottery on the ground and coiled fragments of turkey-feather blankets centuries old slipping into the ground as if ghosts were swirling in this place. They stirred up behind our steps, following us because no one more gullible and obvious was here to follow. Usually we'd check permits at Window Rock. Or better, get someone's okay on the premises, sacks of flour and such, calling from a fence until someone comes out. This isn't the United States with its seas of doorbells, lipstick ladies calling. On the reservation, people know what you're up to before you arrive. You don't make a move without someone seeing it, hearing you were coming, standing outside the door and shaking your hand as if you'd just met, but they'd been watching for days. Families have been in place for centuries. Bloodlines and stories go back thousands of years. Of course people know the moment you step foot on the ground. When I worked with a Navajo archaeologist, visiting rubble mounds and fallen towers many centuries old on the reservation, we had permission from every neighbor, word sent out months before we came. If we hadn't, someone would have stopped in at every site to find out who we were, even with no one around to be seen. You can't hide here.

We didn't veer from Burning Man, figured we'd take a guess at the exclusion boundary, an invisible line on a desert pan, and make a sharp turn when we got there. After we'd made it about half a mile across, as straight a line as we'd been asked not to do, another black truck from another direction started up. They must have had radios.

We'd been watching them since the day before, getting a sense of positions, who could see what. A plane went over every few hours, tracking the playa, a timing we could count on. We were going to try to slip in between overflights and just avoid the ground patrols, but there was no hiding the last few miles. We could see them as clearly as they could see us.

A bigger and darkly bearded man pulled up and said we had to turn here to go around the city site, we had to enter from the other side. Wearing everything we had on our backs, chalked from days of travel, we leaned into his window with our map, saying we had one more legal half mile. Why beleaguer the point? Where they wanted us to go, the back lots of Black Rock City, cranes and empty flatbeds, camps of workers either hurrying to get sculptures out on deck, or artists exhausted and asleep on cots or tarps on the ground, was not where we wanted to be. We'd rather have been in the mash of countless DJs banging at the sky right in front of us. Half a mile, we said, and we're turning sharp right. He shook his head but we had him to rights. We'd run into a couple BLM rangers two evenings before, a set of headlights that found our camp. Big white Ford with sirens, they'd seen us from several miles off, came over to make sure we knew what we were doing with seventy thousand people gathered about ten miles to the south. We explained we were walking in, we had tickets. They gave us their map, explained the boundaries and how far you can go, and left us armed with enough knowledge to face the Black Rock Police with skulls and crossbones on their trucks.

The guy grunted and said okay, but after half a mile he didn't want to see us beelining for the city.

The tracks in snow had a searching quality, like they were looking for something, and I tried not to think it was us. Different size feet: a big waffle stomper and a couple regular guys. Meanwhile, the mountain lion was all over the place. We kept coming on its tracks as we followed canyon to canyon, heading toward an exit, a highway, where we could put out our thumbs and get the hell out of here. In the pointillist light that comes at the end of dusk, I went up the canyon alone to fill water. The air was silently chilled, firs standing tall and round, darkening the canyon bottom. I could have heard a needle drop. I'd stepped into a fairy tale, a dark one, one of Grimms'. What were you supposed to do? Greet an old woman and give her a gift? Don't eat from the banquet table, not even a grape? How many turns to this story had we not even seen, off-rez guys who forgot what country they were in? I quickly gathered water and returned to camp.

If there was ever an illegal alien, I felt like one. I was walking over histories as if the earth were the only history, an error of arrogance and blindness I didn't know I had. Manifest Destiny had thinned until I could see through it, a genocidal publicity stunt, a slogan handed out on fliers to ensure enthusiastic followers. The language I speak is the most recent to be heard around here, arrived at the eleventh hour from an island in a faraway sea, and I'd been speaking it thinking myself a prince, an explorer. Now I was exploring the trenches of a canyon looking for the way out.

In the daylight, we passed palatial cliff dwellings in handsome states of ruin, rubble piles and standing walls, masonry work stacked like books, kiva walls probably plastered and still painted. We were in over our heads. We stopped looking at ruins, stopped ogling them with binoculars. Now it was time to leave, our welcome overstayed since the day we arrived. We were trespassing, though I wasn't sure on whose land exactly or by what authority. That's been the problem from the start, a habit I didn't know I had, an entitlement down in the fine print of my thinking: this land is my land. That I thought I belonged anywhere I want, that if I waved happily people would wave back, was a conceit one does not easily deserve.

I'd thought we were stealthy coming back this deep, that we'd be off all radars, trouble to no one. The earth is a radar. It magnifies your presence, and some are listening. We split up to scout a way through, a choice of left or right in fresh snow, one canyon or the other to get us out. He took right and I took left and we met back where we started an hour or so later, him saying that his way looked good, no prints in the snow, no sign of anyone, we'd be invisible. Within seconds of him telling me this, semi-automatic weapon fire broke out in the canyon he'd just come from, far enough away it didn't drown in its own echoes, close enough to be way too close. We ducked the hell out of there and took the left option.

A new truck came out to greet us after a half a mile, after we weren't veering quite enough. It was a big white vehicle with chrome bumpers, a workhorse from somewhere inside the city. The driver rolled down his window as he stopped beside us. He looked like a retired pro wrestler, long golden hair and mustache, introduced himself with the name of a Norse god, head of security for the city, and asked if his boys had treated us well. We said they had. He glanced at the horizon where we'd come from and told us he sure appreciated what we were doing but we had to stop. There was only one way into Burning Man.

The man explained that they'd been watching us for three days, had a bead on us the whole time by visual and radar. We asked, By radar? He puzzled us for a second, saw the camera gear we carried, tripod and cases, and understood we must have been making some kind of film. That would explain it, he said, because sometimes we were all walking one direction and then we'd all walk another, a camera man getting B-roll in different lighting.

I'll give you an option, the man said. You can either walk all the way around, which I respect, or you can hop in the bed of the truck and I'll take you to the entrance of the city.

We left in a snow storm, the hogan we passed quiet, smoke coming out its pipe. Sheep jangled their bells, hurrying through sweeping ghosts of wind and snow, while the sleek sheepdog watched us pass and hardly looked, didn't bark. It's as if everyone knew what we were up to, working to not impede our efficient exit: here's the door.

In deep forest I've sometimes felt like I can't be seen. If I sit long enough a squirrel forgets why it chattered and I can vanish. On the plains, I sink between rises and draws, and I can lie like grass. But on rock, playa, or jagged ridge, you are seen. There is no hiding. You can go softly, but always someone else is softer. A footprint can last a decade, a broken rock, snapped by a boot step, cracked into three bird's-foot pieces, can last a hundred years or more. Sit on a boulder and flake rock, making a weapon or tool, and the glassy shards might stay in place for a thousand years. There is no invisibility here.

This is why the land must remain, why wilderness can never be dismissed. Whatever is happening in those canyons, twining of tracks and untouched snow, needs to happen. The wild must have a way. It was an accident that my buddy and I showed up, a misunderstanding on our part. We'd walked through the middle of sacred ground, ghosts around us holding their breath. So much was unseen to us, but we could feel it, as if touched by the breeze of shadows. There has to be a place to hide for what is truly wild.

When we reached the highway, light flakes of snow skidded across asphalt. We stuck out our thumbs and eventually a pickup pulled over, a man driving, part Hopi, part Navajo, his family filling the cab. He told us we could jump in. We rode in the back, gloved hands in our armpits, relieved for the way out.

Head of security drove us out with our packs loaded in the bed. With wind in our teeth, sitting against tailgate and wheel wells, we sailed around a playa track, fastest we'd moved in days. Fine, chalky dust rose behind us, and the city lifted from the plain as strangely as a congregation of balanced rocks.

BALANCED ROCKS

The sculptor dropped to his knees and looked beneath a boulder the size of a truck's engine, not a pickup, but a big diesel, a large erratic spalled from somewhere above. He wore a few days' worth of gear, enough water to get him to the next source, a rain hole or a dribble from the rock. He reached his hand under the wind-worn hulk of sandstone, enough space he could form a fist. The boulder's entire mass was being held up by three stones, one the size of a marble, the other two tennis balls at most. The rest of the boulder touched nothing. It seemed to float. The geometry perplexed him. Not that he didn't understand how this had come to be—he did, and that's what perplexed him.

The sparseness is what makes the place, nothing cluttered about it. Even the rock formations that bunch up against each other or the canyons bottomed with boulders are being constantly cleaned, sprayed out, sent downstream and up in the wind, dust devils ripping like ancestors.

The sculptor works mostly out of the Pacific Northwest making large, naturalistic exhibits in museums and public spaces, tearing apart an old wooden schooner to refashion its planks and masts, balancing the vessel on end inside a multi-story space. He has a thing for trees, painstakingly recreating them life-sized, a twisted bristlecone pine, a Guatemalan ceiba, a western hemlock 140 feet tall. The latter project, the tall tree, he was offered a large sum of money to sell. He turned down the advance because after it stops touring, he plans to lay his sculpture, made of a mesh of wooden pieces, on the ground before the original tree in the Cascade Mountains. There, he'd let it slowly sink into earth. He likes the decay of the world, and the world's resistance to it. For him, it is not the object that is so important, but the time the object takes.

He crawled around the boulder, looking under it from every angle, used to estimating weights and balance points, hooking cables and wires. He asked how much I thought the boulder weighed and I ventured a few thousand pounds.

He studied it and agreed. Working with his hands, he knew the weight of rock. He had climbed mountains with ropes, a mix of Indiana Jones and Andy Goldsworthy. He once fell into a glacial crevasse and hung by a climbing rope inside the glassy vault, his partners arresting him up top, anchoring him so that for a moment he floated. He described the shapes he saw, fluted, rounded concavities, expressions of ice, how constructed they were, how organic and flawless.

Here, the same had happened, natural forces wound into the earth, stone feathered by wind and water. The boulder had landed here from a collapse long ago, coming to rest on a bed of other broken rock, each weathering over thousands of years. Detritus had blown and washed away, and only the key structural parts remained, three small rocks evenly holding a few thousand pounds of weight. Delicately and soundly balanced, he said. He shook his head, got back up, and kept walking, having paused for only a moment in the boulder's eddy.

I was taking him out to a region I'd found, a circus of erosion I thought he'd appreciate. This was my backyard, an hour from home and another hour by rough dirt. It is where the land comes apart, kneaded and eaten by canyons, buttes holding fast, but growing smaller by the epoch. Go five miles in any direction across the

Colorado Plateau and you'll find something like this, a slickrock hogback, winding arroyo, a canyon that opens into a giant terrarium, water spattering on stone. You'll find boulders and clay hills, overhangs and naked domes. You want to see erosion and secret holes, this plateau is the sinuous epicenter, its rivers running hard with mud and froth. We were on the Colorado side, slickrock desert pouring into Utah. There is no action here other than erosion. Cities of stone are falling apart, a fact I knew the sculptor would enjoy.

Female earth, male earth; out here, you get it all. The skin of our planet is egalitarian, equally crust and sky, push and pull, elemental dualities fitting into each other like the ribbed wings of an insect.

Laws of attraction and repulsion keep everything in motion. You can't make it twenty or thirty feet without stopping, finding a boulder fallen in two, slid apart as if halved by a sword, the two sides held up by five rocks as tall as coffee-table legs as if it were striding away. You add up winter ice wedges and roots of shadscale or barberry bush that grew in what was once a crack and the tableau seems as possible or impossible as you'd like. The rest is mystery.

At the prow of a canyon-headed mesa overlooking Zion, I found a mature ponderosa pine grown up against soft, yellowed sandstone. Its shelter, the reason it was here, was this slightly overhanging cliff, against which the tree grew. Its entire life was spent pressing into rock, wearing a groove for the trunk and every branch. With every wind, another grain of sand knocked loose by each sway, the tree making a replica of itself, a sculpture in reverse. When it dies and turns to duff, a record will remain in the rock, the image of itself, as if chiseled and sanded smooth.

You could spend a lifetime with calipers registering every fold of this country, finding untold erosional conundrums. You could live a century singing in alcoves listening to your voice bounce back from all directions. And this is only Zion, where a friend woke one morning, looked at the walls soaring around him catching the first light, and said, Go to bed nature, you're drunk.

It is not just one place, but everywhere. Eroded menageries are in the remnant slots of the Glen, hobgoblin Needles, the deeply cupped alcoves of the Waterpocket Fold. Northern New Mexico's Bisti Badlands are worn into ghosts, and Baby Rocks flies by your window on a highway across northern Arizona. My small place in the Colorado desert, an hour's drive from my house, isn't one of the known spectacles, no Zion or Grand Canyon. It is BLM, old mining country, dirt roads, not many cattle, and long, convoluted spaces. Walk around enough and you'll find the sweet spots, secret glens that no one would dare ask you to reveal. There are pebbles on spikes and narrow canyons coiled like eels. I know a place, don't tell anyone, where you slide for a hundred feet through a slot flossed into towering bedrock, some spots too narrow to wear a pack, and it opens into a spacious, secret grotto, a boxed-in park made of fallen boulders, fine-haired grasses, and hackberry trees, like a sultan's private garden.

Intoxication has swerved and swayed across the land, not Paul Bunyan and his axe and ox, but a feathered god, a trickster with a bag full of stars, thrower of the moon, coyote howling and slipping away. The maker of this place informed the backdrops for Road Runner cartoons, ridiculous archways and bowlegged pillars. It was a mad sculptor with uproarious humor and monumental aspirations.

The Colorado Plateau, this exhibit of eroded impracticalities, lies on the meeting of four states: Arizona, Utah, Colorado, New Mexico. It is a gentle dome made of earth pressing up like a newborn's wrinkled head, temporals and parietals hinged against each other, not quite fused. Driven by colliding plates, the buckling crust sends layer after layer of rock skyward at a fraction of an inch per year. In most of the West, you see either lava fields or butchered mountains and basins, fault blocks broken across each other's backs, rock formations a billion years apart grinding against each other. The Plateau is more or less stable in the midst, bobbing on the sea of North America, rock layers mostly unbroken. Because the land is coming up, thirteen thousand feet at its highest, it gives erosion something to chew on, more stone rising from below for whatever rivers and winds want to make of it, making this the decomposing geologic freak show of the West, temples, nipples, chairs, spines, shoulders, buttes, and mesas. Every turn is a little Zen garden, yucca and single-leaf ash held in a smooth bowl of rock, or an Easter egg standing thirty feet tall, a piece of limestone balanced on its tip, a slender toe holding it in place.

This impression of the land is a hunger. I would see ten thousand arches if I could. I would draw them and pin them on the map of my mind. I would be the wind scraping ground, every pass plucking out another grain of sand. I would take lifetimes to scramble and poke, quick heart of a weasel, scanning eye of the vulture. Love of this land is dangerous. It wants more and more. This place would pull you in, like young Everett Ruess exploring the arms of Escalante in the early 1930s, scratching his name in rock, *Nemo*, which means no man, and he was never seen again.

The starkness and elegant decomposition of stone might do this to you. The root of a tree splits a boulder seventy million years old. Fossilized Cretaceous winds and bedding planes are sand-blasted and opened like a book. It's dizzying to watch, even though nothing appears to be moving.

There are palaces of ghosts, cliff dwellings half-ruined and tamped into declivities in Navajo, Cedar Mesa, Chinle formations. Stone People. Centuries ago, ancestors of the Pueblo, Navajo, Ute, Paiute, and others chipped and smoothed steps into cliffs and canyon walls, sometimes deep enough for only a toehold a hundred feet in the air, a dish small enough it might hold a bar of soap. You'd hang the weight of your body on it, and reach for the next step. I imagine their feet nimble, Neolithic Native Americans with fingertips glassed from touching so much rock, their check dams in the canyons built so they could grow corn and raise turkeys, backing up copious sediment to make farm plots. They lived off the soils that flowed in, and the rains that soaked them.

We lost track of each other for long moments, feeling our own ways up the sidewall of a late-day mesa. The routes we picked fit our individual bodies, the reach of our upward stride. What was not rock was juniper, elegant grotesqueries of wood and green sprigs twisted up from the ground, or it was a cluster of yuccas, like armed sea creatures adapted to dry land. Mountain mahogany bushes crowded and redirected till we found each other on top, standing at the edge of cliff that dropped down the other side of the mesa, putting us on a point of rock, bow of a ship, Dolores River squirming and digging at red, solid earth below. We came up here for no better reason than to see. We'd spent part of our day hunting along cliffs for a route to the top, any place that sheer sandstone might let us through, like a cat nosing at the closet door, seeing if it might creak open.

Coming back down, heading for a place to camp for the night, we used fractures and rock-falls, places where bushes had pried slabs apart, places to grab hold and let your body fall, wedging a boot sole, jumping a few feet to the next ledge down. Rock is not trail, is not pathway. If there are railings, they should be used only if needed; they are bush limbs and juniper trunks, not always reliable. The scale is not for you. There is no hierarchy, only parts fitting together, geometry, the mathematical earth. It has nothing to do with the reach of your arm or your step. Ask the climbers, the ones who take big walls and mountains, and the canyoneers who glide like spiderlets on ropes over lips into chasms: these places are not made for us.

We scrambled down the final boulder slopes to where we'd left our packs, and picked them up, carried them farther into the softness of dusk, looking off points of rock into a canyon filled with evermore points of rock, like the retreating teeth of a shark. Bags were spread on the ground. Our stove hissed, dinner fixed, and then darkness filled in. We talked but mostly listened. Rock gives silence in a way that the woods do not. Even the arboreal desert of southern Arizona and Sonora sounds muffled, saguaros and paloverde trees acting as baffles. On the rock, sound doesn't stop. It flies away. The clank of a pan echoes through flat-faced rocks and cliffs.

We chose our own places to sleep, the sculptor on a broad, flat ledge blocked from wind, me on the other side of the point, offered out to the canyon as if sleeping on a bowsprit. I don't know his last thoughts as he drifted off under his slight rock overhang, but mine were of the flatness beneath my back, which wasn't really flat, more like a roughly made bed of solid stone, naked as the ball of a bone. I fell asleep to a pebble I'd neglected to sweep away, size of a walnut pressing into my back and my sides as I rolled through the night, back and forth, but not off my pad, not into the canyon far below, just enough to rock my dreams to sleep.

For the last couple decades, the sculptor and I had been exchanging occasional gifts in the mail, me sending him the gray-skinned ghost of a paper wasp nest, him sending me an odd coil of rusted metal. We'd never met in person. This was our first time. He'd been trying deserts lately, getting out of trees. His last exploration had been Craters of the Moon in southern Idaho, a barren rock-scape of bulging, cresting lava several thousand years old. He said he was seeing as much life in rock as he was in trees. I said I knew just the place, two-day-long platforms of sandstone I'd found on the outskirts of Paradox Valley in southwestern Colorado.

I could have taken him to the goblin fields of the San Rafael Swell in Utah. The caprocked towers of the Sierra Ancha in Arizona, sedimentary books stacked skyward. The Chiricahua Mountains with their caves like earlobes and open mouths a hundred feet tall. Anyplace would do, arroyos shaped like snakes leaving archways and pedestaled rocks, a chain of steeples, a devil's shoulder, pelvis, spine. Just a stroll around Arches National Park would have been almost too much, like putting a flash bomb in his face. I imagine what he would say, coming over a rise onto Delicate Arch, a rock formation that looks more like a giant's daintiest bones than anything geologic. We would have looked on with fifty or a hundred others, most in silence, all having paid their fee to get in, standing and sitting in a powerful contemplation of what is even possible in this world. He would have said it looked as if gods had lived here when earth was made of clay, the only way such a thing could ever happen. I would say I wouldn't be surprised if one day geologists broke down and finally admitted they'd known all along that the geometry of Delicate Arch and many of the other arches and balanced rocks in the area was physically impossible. They were formed through no known geologic process, evidence of divine hand, proof at last.

What people might not get is that geology *is* the hand of God. The wind is God's breath, and water carries it all away.

Neither the sculptor nor I were religious. If anything, our shared religion was growth, decay, and the contours formed between. Evidence of the divine is beside the point. Have you seen a hummingbird nest hung on a string of flood debris in a desert wash? Or the echoing marks of conchoidal fractures on a rock face a hundred feet tall, where long ago a giant slab broke free? You can see the very center where the rock snapped open, a shell-shaped pluck.

I knew he'd enjoy this zone in western Colorado, boulders perched, slickrock endless. He smiled, fascinated, walking round and round a near-toppled formation, fingering blowholes made by wind and placing both hands on the belly of the rock, pregnant he said, feeling as if for the fetus inside. Bringing him here was my gift; it would all be too much to send in the mail.

High desert stretches you, contorts and spirals your limbs. Hairy bark appears between your wood, and fingers grow into many. The berries you make are hard and sky blue, falling to the ground like pearls, like rough jewels, more than enough to string around your neck. It's the presence of thirst and the finding of water, the beating sun, the wind that strips you bare.

It won't happen on your first trip, or in a hundred trips, or from coffee-table books or helicopter flights. It happens slowly, every time, whenever you glance to the desert, or when you open a sleeping bag and sand comes out. It happens in the middle of the day far away, taking off your sunglasses in the city and looking up, reminded somehow of the dimensions of a canyon. Once you see the planet falling into pieces over and over, you realize the constant workings of nature, and they are everywhere. You feel the tension in the air of elements perforated, caught mid-collapse between rise and fall.

You can't help but applaud as it all comes apart. We love the debris plumes, fireworks, and dust. Who wouldn't watch a great ship sinking, soul shuddering at the sight? This is what you feel in these worn and defiant shapes, the entire world splitting open, as if Earth were alive, dying to be reborn.

It all comes apart, but not all at once. Variations in timing and shape create this country. We knocked down a few rocks just getting out of camp that morning, jumping over cracks, scrambling up the other side. We used the shade of a twisted desert juniper to stop and have breakfast, quick yogurts and nuts, as the sculptor eyed the tree like he'd eyed so many parts of this desert, thinking about how painful and gorgeous it all is, how hard the environment presses on living things, how it drives them toward oblivion, and they press back. The beer can, the bullet, the shape is what remains, a juniper crucified against the sky, much of it dead, abandoned long ago, while green, scaly sprays are still erupting from new branches, a breath of life.

We packed up and moved along slickrock benches, exploring in and out of bread loaves and seep-haunted overhangs. There was an object I wanted him to see. I stayed back, letting him find for himself a balanced boulder that would elsewhere require a park sign, maybe a fence around it so that nobody taps on it and finds a rock the size of a bathroom fallen on them.

He knew what I was up to when he saw it far off; you couldn't miss this one, a boulder longer than both our reaches combined, piece of cliff or rocky overburden tumbled here long ago and angled down a gentle slope as if in the act of sliding, falling off. But it does not move. It is raised chest-high off the ground by a tuffet of bedrock. Ducking under and looking closely, he saw only a few points of contact, a nut of a rock and little passages blown through the sedimentary underside by wind, making it appear as if five fingers or fewer were being used to hold up a boulder that must have weighed a hundred tons. He walked underneath it in the circle of its shade.

We took different vantages, sitting apart from each other, standing together, engaging like set directors pointing this way and that, discussing where the rock's center lay, how the axis of weight, though it looked terribly lopsided, ran through the mass and directly down into a bedrock neck the boulder had made for itself, a thing to stand on. He asked about time and I told him it was hard to tell, that it could be standing for ten thousand years more, or it could fall tomorrow. How long had it been here, he wondered, and I took in the curve of slickrock I'd been tromping around on for decades, bantering with scientists, looking at geologic maps and historically repeated photography where sometimes this land doesn't appear to change at all, a hundred years and no boulder has moved. I told him it probably landed in the early Pleistocene, a few hundred thousand years ago, maybe longer. Based on the way it's angled, like a boat being pushed off a dock into the water, it landed on an angled surface to begin with and has remained tilted to this day. The rest of the sandstone beneath it, everything around it, has deflated, worn off by three hundred thousand years or more of weather, leaving a point to stand on.

When I was younger, I thought this country must have been made by a giant flood. Noah wasn't on my mind, just scale and complexity. What could have caused so much to fall apart so thoroughly, as if the land were crumbling into itself? Stepping foot into it, following canyon bottoms and scree fans, I began to understand the time involved, rainstorms, flash floods, and dust-scoured rock. Boulders crashed, ledges collapsed, and platforms snapped underfoot. Entropy was having its heyday.

If it had been catastrophic, formed in a single event as I once surmised, the canyons would not be as gently shaped and this boulder would not be balanced. It would have washed away with everything else, leaving mountainous junk piles of debris across the Southwest, where no evidence of such a flood exists. What does exist is wind and rain, the gradual pry of winter ice, the open hole of gravity. The land does not move to our eyes, but it shrinks and grows, yawns and stretches.

The more I studied, the more I felt the heat of earth as equal partner to erosion, ancient asteroid impacts and a radioactive core effervescing. If it were only decay, only levelness would remain, everything filled in. Internal, planetary heat gives this desert half its shape, sending the land up against the sky. As if spun on a potter's wheel, the clay presses back against the hand. Resistance is not futile; it is required.

One law of thermodynamics states that all warm things in a closed system will inevitably become cold, thought to be the way of the entire universe. But all is not cold. Other forces are at work, heat welling and rising. No system is ever closed. It is the gape of gravity and the upward thrust of tectonics, pistons pumping, thrust and fall, rain and sun, moon and ice. Constant tension is written into everything, moving from the cold to the hot and back.

On the ground, it feels as if rock is dripping into the sky. Boulders bloom and rise like orbs in a lava lamp, while others cool and sink. You see this in the sculptor's work, blossoms and air holes, life and earth folded together. He called a piece "Murmur." I saw it in a museum in Anchorage,

Alaska, an installation the size of a small ball-
room, his re-creation of an Arctic hillock you
could walk inside of, the top mechanically open-
ing and closing over your head as if the landform
were a flower unfurling. He'd named it after a
murmuration of birds, a flock flying together like
a shoal of fish, creating shapes in the air that are
gone the moment they are formed. The flocks, he
said, were ephemeral, elegant, moving, the same
as the earth. If our eyes had the patience of mil-
lennia, we'd see.

This is what he saw at the edge of Colorado,
walking across whale bellies, getting up next to
a mushroom-headed pillar of sandstone tall as a
person and a half, bizarre pieces of construction
left behind. Deeper timeframes were passing for
him, longer nows, earth's surface swelling and
receding like flocks of birds. We walked for the
rest of the day as stiff, warm winds poured across
us, howling and snapping, sending us to camp in
the leeward side of a butte. We used its overhangs
and backsides of boulders as shelter.

There wasn't much talking in the wind. We
could hear strands of it threading over rock,
whistling, inhaling, gushing, but not each other.
The sculptor laid his bag on bare rock where the
wind wasn't so bad. I went off with a flashlight
to find my own place. The side of the butte had
eroded into fingers, little washes wide enough to

take my shoulders, each one starting with a faint
overhang, enough I could have nuzzled out of the
wind. The first shelter had a black widow spider
hanging in the middle, as did the second, the
third, and the fourth. Their webs were messy and
many-stranded, built in windbreaks, little bays
with plenty to anchor to. Each spider was a glass
marble with a red hourglass on the abdomen.
Tips of stiletto legs held it from invisible threads.
Hanging unaware of me, not flinching at my
headlamp, they were perfectly poised, their kills
suspended around them like amulets. The spiders
come out at night and sense the web, feeling for
the struggle of prey. I tried not to trip the strands
as I walked one to the next. I didn't want to send
them scrambling for their cracks where they'd
hide among papery moons of egg sacks.

I laid my bag out in the wind, away from the
spiders. Settled head to toe along the grain of the
wind, I listened to sand rush and swish against
nylon. Outside, the land felt violent, tossed by the
air, wearing badly.

BADLANDS

There's a scrappy little piece of desert where I used to take refuge. Locals call it the *dobes*—pronounced doe-bees—for its cracked and powdered clays. You can make adobe bricks out of the stuff, add water and straw and pour the slick, grainy mixture into wooden molds for building a house or bunker. Fossil shells shine across these rolling badlands and sparsely scattered sage. This part of western Colorado, between one small town and another, is the bottom of a shallow Cretaceous sea lifted up to about six thousand feet at the edge of the southern Rockies, drylands where little more than shadscale and sage grow in bitter soils. I lived near one of the towns, population five hundred, for almost two decades. Our place was up higher in a valley where my family had snow most of the winter. Down here, the soil would freeze hard like crystal. Light frost gathered around the entrances to rodent burrows, speaking to small mammals sleeping inside.

I came to dry scarps and hard-panned wash bottoms in the dobes when I needed to get away from the house, a fifteen-minute drive to this patch of drought and few trees. I called it my desert, my asylum. Most people knew it as the place where couches get dumped and you have to be careful of errant bullets fired by crazy rednecks. For me, it was the feeling of big sky and nothing in the way. The feeling of one step and another touching ground, no sound but the crush of soil and breathing. It was the best, closest desert I could find.

A desk had been left on an ad hoc shooting range down a rutted two-track. I'd take my computer and set up at this metal desk as long as my battery allowed, pulling up a folding chair, plank of splintered wood for a seat, stacking reference books around me. The desk was here for sighting rifles, a stable base for calibrating long-range weapons to knock out markers fifty yards across a trashy expanse of blown-up propane bombs, bottles, cans, a couple former televisions, and whatever else anyone had set out as targets.

Shooters would come while I was working. We'd usually have a good talk. Some explanation was needed. Books, deadlines, kids at home, you know the routine. They'd pull out their arsenals. One man I knew from the town of Crawford, where my kids went to school. He was a wiry, sun-worn white guy in his fifties, both of us out here for a desert fix. He said you can breathe out here, nothing hidden. He spread out weapons on his tailgate, a couple of handguns, a semi-automatic rifle. He said he'd leave the sweetheart in its padded case for now, a long-range firearm. He said he could pick off an ear from a thousand yards, and that when the civil war came, his place just down the road is where I wanted to be.

I thought it possibly wasn't, but it was good to know he was around. I asked if he kept penicillin in the refrigerator. He laughed, no. He was doing it the hard way. I said maybe I'd bring some down to him if worse came to worse. We're all preppers out here. It'd be dumb not to be. This is a far, dry place where it's good to have extra beans and gas for the generator. Maybe that's why he and I had a thing for these barren hills and junk piles. Out here, you're on your own.

Hunters dump carcasses in the dobes. Hill-tops and road-ends are bone fields, elk with their heads sawed off, and deer once supple now torn by coyotes and eagles. I take myself on osteology tours out there, nudging over ribs or a spine with a boot sole to see how old they've grown in the

ground. You become a forensic student. Wipe off
a deer scapula that's been on the ground a decade
and use it as a fan, not a scent to it. Dog carcasses
get hauled into these hills, little yappers the size of
raccoons, and bigger ones the size of bay hounds.
Most looked old, teeth worn down from the years.
Work dogs, I guessed, tossed in the desert instead
of buried.

In a strange way, I felt at home with litter and
bones and big stretches of not much of anything.
I'm nostalgic, maybe the way New Yorkers far
from home might think wistfully on the odor of
a summer garbage strike in the city, black, stink-
ing trash bags stacked into mountains in front of
buildings. Not only the beautiful parts are cher-
ished; grotesqueries have their own rooms to ex-
plore.

Growing up around Phoenix, Arizona, I saw
where people ditched old computer equipment
and fridges, blasted them with shotguns, nipped
and pierced them with bullets. A couch dumped
in the desert is a kind of species. You'd put it on
a checklist. Then a television. A fridge. Bonus for
a bathtub or a dumped porta potty. I used to find
cars, but not so much anymore. They're worth
something now, and made of too much plastic to
make shooting any fun. I remember them burned
and shot up, parts pulled out, metal rusting, win-
dows bashed in with rocks. I'd look for coins, a

matchbook, a receipt, anything that suggested People Who Came Before. It wasn't that the desert was absolutely covered with trash. Just in a ring around the city, and up against the inner-urban mountain ranges, focused around two-tracks and washes, people too lazy to get it out farther. Not so much trash like paper cups and beer cans, these were more like reference points, objects chosen for their size, weight, or shape. A refrigerator alone on a hill, shot by firearms from every side, was a lone monument.

South side of Phoenix, I noticed, had more bathtubs. One had been planted upright like a niche, and the Virgin of Guadalupe had been painted inside in resplendent colors, her head tipped in benevolence, absolving us of all that we've done. Even that had a few bullet craters, rusty circles punched into porcelain but not making it through.

My dad and I would go out and shoot the crap out of things. I loved our weekends. Nobody around for miles, the desert was ours. I grew up lucky with the West's public lands. He'd load a rifle or two in the truck, a shotgun, a couple handguns. We'd line up bottles, set out old car batteries, or anything left on a desert floor of creosote and gangly ocotillo that hadn't already been obliterated. We'd fire an afternoon of rounds. As a kid, I was allowed to use the .22 rifle or the .410, while he blew off his cannon of a .357, a thing that scared me. When he offered to let me try, I said no. I didn't want to get close to that kind of power.

You wouldn't do this in the woods. There are things you can't see, people and animals out there. In these open places, you see just about everything that happens, Gila woodpeckers looking over saguaro tops at us, crying as they'd dive away.

The litter in the desert is a confession, and shooting at it drives the point home. We are marking our place, like handprints at the mouth of a canyon, saying don't screw with us, we live here, this desert is ours. It's a redneck sensibility, a dangerous one, but good to have at your side.

In the dobes, I knew of a couple washing machines, one fridge—the usual. I used them as landmarks, the way back to an arroyo that carved a tunnel-arch, a route to the powerlines. I know it's not right, I should have taken these things to the dump or to recycling, stripped them for parts, turned them into art, a planter, anything. I've got friends who come out with empty trailers and load up for the dump, and I think it's a good thing, but my landmarks go missing. They took the five-gallon bucket I'd dug up from being half-buried and turned upside down so I could sit on it and watch the sky.

* * *

Have you walked the bombing ranges with their missile traces and Thunderdome dogfights? Have you shielded the sun with your hand, nipped by the shadow of a jet you hadn't heard coming, half a second before the air explodes and it feels like your muscles might tear free of your skeleton? The plane flies off near the speed of sound and you start to breathe again. It is small and far away, its roar dragged like a cape until the desert returns to silence.

Violence and the deepest peace you've ever felt are right up against each other. Most of my time on the Barry M. Goldwater Range in southern Arizona, researching water holes and leaving my truck outside the boundary under a camouflage tarp, I spent in blissful emptiness. Opened in 1941 for aerial and air-to-ground combat testing, the range is still being used for the same purpose: strafing and rocket delivery. From all these years of use, saguaro-dotted bajadas are decorated with brass and rusty metals from targets and projectiles. I found spent warheads, small, tubular rockets, and, once, the crater of a crashed jet, its important parts trucked off while wires and gray rivets remained, glass melted to powder.

We've used the desert as a punching bag, its surface pocked and riddled with hostilities. If these desert airspaces were not military, would we still be fighting in Afghanistan? Are wars where they are because we began practicing in dry expanses of empty sand washes and isolated, naked ranges?

On the bombing ranges I saw no sign of humans on the ground more recently than centuries ago. Brown and buff pottery makers, flintknappers, people who pecked bighorn sheep and shell imagery into cliffs and boulders. It was more wilderness than most wildernesses, trammeled by man, certainly, but only from the sky. On the ground, I saw no one for many days in all directions.

Though the desert could feel angry—mountains jagged, most living things clawed, spiked, or poisonous—the only turmoil I sensed was in the impact craters and empty weapon shells. We'd brought the violence with us. It is not inherent to the desert.

A giant amber wasp dragged away a paralyzed but breathing spider, and I felt none of the wrath or exhilarating release that must come from dropping a five-hundred-pound bomb. Instead, it felt like work on the wasp's part. It felt like survival, no rage or moaning philosophies. Completely apolitical at a time when the way you breathe is political. Even with its rusting, rotting artifacts, the desert is my retreat from the madness. I'd take a day by foot, or a month by meandering washes with ironwood and ragweed scratching in the wind, over a dizzying flight near the speed of sound, my brain slugging back in my skull at the strain of a hard turn, carrying enough missiles under the wings to level ten hospitals.

Violence in the desert is not hidden by blackberry brambles or tucked back in the woods. It is out for all to see.

The sound of wind blowing through saguaro needles will bring you to a standstill, something I remember from the bombing range.

Place your open hands on the trunk of the cactus, gently, because its spines are sharp. Give them enough weight that your palms begin to prickle, but not so they puncture or bleed. Standing still, you will feel the invisible sway of the tall cactus. Stand longer and you'll feel every needle singing through your hands, reverberating along the trunk. This might balance out a jet flight, a grain on this side of the scale, a wish for peace and subtlety.

Metal monsters stand one after the next in the dobes, carrying high-tension power lines that crackle and hiss for miles. They truss one horizon to the next. I half adored and half hated the pylons and their bright, arcing wires.

Alone, out of the house on a blustery afternoon, I walked along with the monsters, pausing at each cross-barred structure, standing where all the lines came together ahead of me, lines match-

ing lines, like stepping through a cathedral ceremony, smoke of incense swaying back and forth
under passageways of flawless symmetry. I saw
something hanging from a piece of twine tied to
a metal L-bar. I walked over and found a naked
Barbie hogtied and tilting in the breeze. Her legs
were bent over her back, her arms bound to her
knees. Her throat was tied back to her arms and
legs, causing her head to crane.

She'd been cut with a sharp implement, a ra-
zor or a honed blade. The plastic between her legs
was horribly gouged. I immediately began to un-
tie her. One more second of her hanging was too
long.

Monster truck, I thought; a guy from town
who couldn't keep his anguish inside. It could
have just as easily been a Subaru rattling down a
two-track to get here, some distraught and furious
lover, someone told *no*, told *don't*, told *you aren't*.

Darkness lies in all sorts of hearts. A woman
could have done the torturing and left the poor
doll here, any gender has the capacity, but that
didn't enter my mind. Out of hand, I believed it
was a man, the current go-to for violent behavior.

Outside the desert is a bigger desert of shot-up
things: schools and dance venues, people who are
hated by a gunman, or people the gunman didn't
think twice about before spraying them against
a wall or small desk. The shooters are invariably

men. Not enough good, open breathing, I think. Not enough sky. Too many bullies, too many people with voices shouting over each other, jeering for position. Too little compassion. Too hurt a world.

We take out fantasies and furies on the land because it's bigger than us and we think the ground can handle it. We think no one hurts when we lay it here. With its sunken, solid batholiths, its bulky mountain ranges rooted into the mantle of earth, unspeakable tonnage of rock and sand at the surface, volcanoes going off and rivers rumbling, it's the biggest thing we can touch. I have held onto boulders with all of my life, letting rock grains soak up whatever horror or odium I dragged with me. The land absorbs. Fracturing fluids cracking open the crust for natural gas, pipes leaking into rivers, residents moving into new desert subdivisions signing Hold Harmless Agreements because their water is limited and not fit to drink. You wonder how much, really, can be absorbed.

Untwining the Barbie's wrists from her legs, I apologized out loud, saying no one deserves this. She had been firmly trussed and when she was free, she unfolded in my hand, her legs and arms coming back, her slender neck straightening, head returning to its attentive, resting self.

I cleared a space on the ground. I could feel her relief, or mine, as I laid her on crusty adobe soil. It was a small thing, not enough to push against the tide, but if every Barbie were untied, peace might be the dominant force. Maybe it already is, but doesn't make headlines, not as showy as turbulence. I left her looking up at the sky, her eyes open, a faint smile still visible on her face. She watched charcoal storm clouds cross over crackling, electrified landlines.

LANDLINES

Every step you take has already been taken.
Every story has already been told. The land
is not newly discovered, so old with legends you
might mistake them for rocks. Changing Woman
whispers in your ear and you think it's only wind.

I stood at the edge of a kiva, arm pointing
north, making a compass needle of myself. The
excavation was extensive, the kiva at least forty
feet across. It was a twelfth-century early Pueblo
site pulled out of the dust and rubble of northwest
New Mexico, tarps over trenches, sifting screens
at the edge of the dig. I was checking alignments,
believing people had built this great ceremonial
chamber like a dial. What was it set to?

Histories stand in these rocks. Mountains have names, legends about when they last got up on their feet and strode across the earth, unleashing mystic arrows, defeating enemies in battle, before lying down and returning to sleep. You can't pass anywhere through the Four Corners without seeing sagas on the horizon. The San Juan River meanders through the middle of it, and through Farmington, where people for many centuries have aligned their lives and architecture toward landmarks and the stories told about them. I walked around the circle of this kiva, stopping over niches in the walls revealed by excavation. At each niche, I scanned the horizon, seeing if there was a line, a point, something they wanted a person to see.

I called out a question. North-south? A few people looked up. I was talking to a Navajo archaeologist standing on the other side of the kiva. He and I were teaching a field program in northwest New Mexico, guiding participants, mostly retired folks, around the pre-contact southern San Juan Basin. Day three: dig site south of the sprawling town of Farmington, New Mexico. The archaeologist moved over to a half-buried masonry door on the due-north pole of the kiva and looked my way, seeing if I gunsighted onto a rock-art panel or a granary built in the cliff behind me. From my vantage, the archaeologist due north marked a flat-topped hill several miles away, its roof sprouting radio towers. You wonder if this is a key, an ancient Pueblo cipher, or if everything aligns with everything.

At dusk, we drove to the high point we'd sighted along the kiva's axis. We didn't expect to find archaeological sites, but we were proving a point: you can see everything out here. This desert is made of high spots, like Mayan temples sticking up from a jungle canopy, all looking at each other. Archaeologists have deciphered a framework of sites and signal stations across this desert basin, and the radio tower hill may have been one. It stood over Farmington on the other side of the muddy San Juan from the kiva. We positioned ourselves, sighting the location of the kiva we'd visited earlier in the day. Beyond that, buttes and rock tips stood fifty miles away. The staggering form of Shiprock rose in the west. Red lights glowed on and off as we drifted around our hilltop, conversations breaking the high desert quiet.

Years ago, my dad told me I was conceived in the town below. My mom's parents lived in Farmington at the time. The Vietnam War was on, and he said my mother whispered his draft number into his ear. That was that. My mom, who was divorced within a few years, said not to believe everything my dad said. My grandparents did live here, though. Judging by the imaginary line between the hilltop and the kiva, and the much smaller size of Farmington in August of 1967, the summer of love when high school sweethearts from a New Mexico desert town got together, the bedroom may have been within view.

Perhaps this is what the kiva builders had intended centuries ago, seeing how our stories and theirs go together, setting up an alignment for people to attend to, walking out and back, sewing the land with memory. My appearance, possibly springing to life somewhere in this town, was another strand in a tapestry woven every day, stacking up for thousands of years, a particular thread or dye, a drop, a stain.

We had two vans with us. The Navajo archaeologist took one and I took the other as we headed south, turning on marked and unmarked Indian roads. Clients were mostly older folks, aiming for ruined villages on the reservation, citadels of mid-Pueblo age, dating to the time of Mesoamerican empires and the Neolithic metropolis of Cahokia near the confluence of the Mississippi and Missouri Rivers, when America was only Native America.

The archaeologist called back on the radio, saying that we needed to stop at a long and solitary butte coming up on our left, an orphan standing on a rolling plain of sandstone and shale, blackbrush and sage.

I knew the butte, so I was surprised. We hadn't planned a stop and I'd never heard anything about the place. I'd camped on top of it once, but I didn't think it stood out for any other reason, except for a cluster of radio and cell towers built on top. We had been able to see the towers from our hilltop in Farmington. If you wanted a view, there was nowhere else to camp.

I remembered years earlier looking out from the roof of the butte, seeing other lines of sight as far away as Colorado and Arizona, mountaintops and points of rock, tightening the focus on my binoculars, seeing Utah, a mirage of the Bears Ears. This butte probably had an archaeological site somewhere, only twenty miles from Chaco Canyon, one of the largest, most complex archaeological regions in North America. I was curious what the archaeologist had to say about it.

He got everyone into a half-circle under the butte with its crumbled flanks and its pallid caprock, its roof stemmed with radio towers, and told us this was considered a starting place for his people, the Diné. He told us Changing Woman was born up there, raised on the butte-top by First Man and First Woman, who made this their first home.

I was surprised to be hearing a story that sounded familiar, as if I'd participated in it. Man, woman, and child in this place. I'd camped on the flat head of this butte with my wife and our infant son years earlier. I had known none of this. I wanted him to back up, to answer a few questions, but the participants were listening eagerly.

Changing Woman, daughter of First Man and First Woman, eventually gave birth to twins who would make the world safe by killing monsters that ruled over the land. When she was older, Changing Woman created the ancestors of the Navajo. This butte is where she is said to have first appeared, an infant swaddled in soft buckskin.

I'd been with a diapered baby up there, bedded in sleeping bags, but I hadn't been present for this older story. I was a late passerby, a happenstance. My family is from a nation outside of this one, whose stories are older than I.

She met me on a dirt road on the reservation, baby in the car seat. I was on foot coming up from Chaco in the scarped and rolling washes of the lower San Juan Basin, oily little springs, small camps, no stove, days of hearing only footsteps and the thoughtful drift of wind. She swept me away in our truck, taking a rough, low four-track up the back side of a butte, access to a cluster of radio towers where we thought we'd camp. I was writing about alignments at the time, ground-truthing what I'd heard from archaeologists about ancient people in this basin connecting each other across long distance lines of sight. The land was made into spiderwebs, strands connecting one place to another, their architecture lined up to stars and mountains.

A September thunderstorm rolled in that night, a sizzling wave of ozone and discharged ions. Swift and violent storms are common that time of year, pillars of cumulonimbus floating like cities over the desert, ready to unleash. We finished dinner and battened down gear, ready for a furious rain. The baby I passed in to his mother, who took him through tent flaps and opened her shirt one-handed.

I hadn't known at the time, but a wild storm with black clouds, rain, and lightning is said to have descended on this butte. The story I'd eventually hear told of First Man thinking the storm was a sign, so he went up top where he discovered a baby in buckskin. That is how First Man and First Woman became parents of the baby girl who would grow up to be Changing Woman.

The only story I knew at that moment was my own, hurrying to beat the storm. I checked stakes, looked to the blue flashes almost on us, and ducked in, zipping the tent closed behind me.

The tent felt like a lifeboat that night. Weather fiercened and lightning struck the top of the butte with a back-rattling boom. Rain fell hard. Male rain, as it's known in Navajo. Driving, swift, flood-making. The radio towers seemed to be drawing the electricity, taking the brunt, protecting us on the ground where we would have otherwise been targets.

When we got up the next morning, the air was crisp and rarefied, storm long gone. Our baby nuzzled at his mama's breast as we looked across what seemed like a newborn land. We were in view of that little hill with radio towers in Farmington thirty miles away, and the rim of Mesa Verde in Colorado forty beyond that. Shiprock stood sixty miles northwest like a beacon.

The Navajo archaeologist, when I told him about what happened to us—the storm, my wife, the baby—laughed and said that it's taboo, you're not supposed to go to the top of the butte. I told him I had no idea. We hadn't seen a sign or gate, not clear if it was Native American land or federal land or a cherry stem to private radio towers, like much of New Mexico—big, open, wild country with barbed wire fences and dirt tracks to follow. He said that the storm homed in on us probably because we were up there. We were lucky we had protection, he said.

I don't know what he meant by protection, maybe radio towers to draw off the lightning, maybe something else.

I remember a close bolt of lightning and my eyes being open, half a second before the air split open, ground thumping with thunder. In that flash-blinding moment, I saw a woman with dark, braided hair curled around a child, and my arm around them both, a nesting of spoons, the same configuration of skeletons found around the world—cities buried in earthquakes or volcanic flow, bones over bones of man, woman, and child, as if a family made a seed of themselves.

This could have been the very place where First Man and First Woman cupped around their only child at the beginning of the world. Our bodies may have fit the space like we belonged here, like beans set back in their pod.

The light snapped to darkness and I did not see its aftermath, the infant startled by the burst and the terrible crash that followed, the hand on the back of his head pulling him in and whispering *hush*.

After the archaeologist told the story, I got back in our van a little stunned, driving away wondering if there are happenstances in the land, places where stories repeat themselves. It is where the air changes density, where we stroll through ghosts. We step into line hardly knowing.

My phone went off in a Farmington hotel that night, the vibrating alarm of a public alert, a child abduction. I checked it on the nightstand, after two in the morning, reading glasses fumbled onto my face. An eleven-year-old Navajo girl went missing in the town of Shiprock, about thirty miles from here. A maroon van was involved, a few descriptions. I sent out a half-hearted, not-quite-awake hope for the girl, whoever she was, trusting she'd be discovered safe and sound.

Had I known what I do now, I should have woken everyone, shouting down the hotel hallway, banging on doors. I would have taken the keys to our van and driven the back roads incessantly. People should have been shouting and clapping, calling in the desert, a wall of flashlights and voices sending out her name.

The alert system in the county had failed. There'd be lawsuits and admissions that money had been squandered, the system not fully in place that night. By the time the alert went out, the girl was harmed beyond repair at the foot of Shiprock, the most striking landmark in the basin, and we were asleep.

In the morning, we drove an Indian road west toward the hulk of Shiprock, a twenty-seven-million-year-old volcanic neck standing 1,500 feet above the desert plain, a ragged-headed god splintered by erosion. It is not an easy landmark to look at. It seems violent, like something stabbed up through the ground. With its long walls of eroded, radiating dikes, it appears to be a huge catch in the middle of a spider's web, or like the castle of a demon king. Anything you name carries something dark.

I'd forgotten about the abduction alert and was turned backwards from the front passenger seat, explaining something about floodplain farming to full bench seats, when the van slowed. The driver asked, What's this?

People were off the sides of the road, their figures dwindling for a mile in both directions. Lines of them, chains crossed over dry, treeless hills and into washes. Cases of water bottles came off a flatbed into people's arms. White people, Native people, disparate colors and kinds of clothing, people with sunhats, people without, a velvet purple dress.

As we slowed, I asked the driver if he got the alert last night. He said he did. As we rolled through, we both wondered if we should stop the vans and get out to help. But they didn't need a geriatric search party adding to their task. We drove on, quietly now, me not explaining anything in the van because I was holding my breath.

In the other van, the archaeologist had been telling a traditional Navajo story about Shiprock, how long ago, monsters ruled the earth and people were here, too, but it was dangerous and people were killed and eaten. Monster Bird lived on Shiprock, and would fly down to capture people in their regalia. Zuni, Ute, Tewa, it didn't matter, no one was spared. They'd be flown over the top of Shiprock, which is said to have been covered with spear points sticking up. Dropped from a great height, their bodies were skewered on landing, blood running down the spears. These victims were food for Monster Bird's chicks.

I don't know where the archaeologist was in the story when we drove through the search parties, but somehow he finished it, because when we pulled over on a dirt side road along a radiating dike tied straight to the rock, and we set up folding chairs for a lecture, he asked one of the participants to recite the story in full. He said it's important to know how to listen and remember, and that speaking takes more of your body than just remembering or writing it down. His father had told him you have two eyes and two ears, just one mouth. You should look and listen more, not just talk. That is how you learn a story and how you are able to tell it.

An older white gentleman recited the story of Shiprock and Monster Bird mostly the way he'd heard it. The archaeologist helped him along, a small detail, the regalia of a Zuni man. We heard about Changing Woman's two twin sons, Monster Slayer and Born of Water, who came to rid the world of terrible beasts. Their story is Homeric, lightning bolts and interceding gods, foibles and failures. It would take winters to tell the whole thing. Monster Slayer, as I heard it told, went to the rock to fight Monster Bird and Born of Water remained behind, instructed to care for a set of sacred sticks. If the sticks caught fire, he was to come help his brother, possibly a reference to fire signals used across this territory a thousand years ago when pueblos and masonry great houses broke the horizon. In the end, Monster Bird was killed and the world was made safe for people, leaving Shiprock to stand as evidence, what is called *Tsé Bit'a'í*, the winged rock.

As the story was told, I stood behind the circle of chairs, looking down the line at Shiprock, hoping over and over for the girl to be found, for a mother to drop everything and run for her, arms outstretched.

If there was a time for a miracle, this was it. But I saw ATVs converging, I saw a person running toward something far away. I saw the end.

Her body was discovered not far from us, left on the dirt. The killer who'd kidnapped her was a Native man from the town of Waterflow, between Shiprock and Farmington. He'd been a stranger who picked up the girl and her younger brother at a bus stop, giving them a ride because she'd hurt her ankle and he said he'd get her home.

That's what he said after he was apprehended at a sweat lodge on the reservation, that she kept saying she wanted to go home.

Her brother escaped and reached the nearest paved road, the one we'd driven in on. The alert that went out became snared in a broken system, not heard until it was too late. A line was snagged, busted, dropped on the ground.

Places remember their history. Every high point gathers stories at its feet. This is where I run out of science. There is something that does not receive or emit light, something you can't see, but you sense, like wind that blows around you, urging you one direction or another. The presence of these stories is made tangible by the places where they happened.

I've been seeing Shiprock all my life, a childhood horizon from when I knew nothing about it, neither volcano nor legend. Its shape will always be in my eyes, a tall ship lumbering across the desert, or, on summer days with cumulus heads behind it, a Pueblo rain god. It stands as a death marker, a dark stone raised for a girl who died on pale red dirt atop ages of ruined room blocks and pueblos a thousand years old. Woven together, stories of this place are endless, strand over strand. The girl now courses through the monsters and the hero twins who slayed them. Her story is part of the pantheon.

I don't know how you walk away from what happened here. I don't think it's possible, or that you should. For some weavers, a strand would not be removed once it's in the rug, even if marked with blood. I kept wondering, what can a person do?

I returned on a day after late-winter rains and soaking sleet. Off the paved two-lane, near where it passes through a break in one of Shiprock's long, rocky dikes, I dug a hole in moist ground at the fence-line. I buried a handful of small, papery bulbs. Come spring, with enough rain, white lilies might grow and blossom, standing as brightly as shells against red soil.

SHELL

In a wash south of Phoenix, I found a crescent moon in the sand, part of a *Glycymeris* shell carved and polished into a bracelet. This kind of artifact had been worn on the arms of women who lived on hilltop villages, bringing their finery out for ceremonies and ball court days in an ancestral city. The artifact was broken in half and worn down, smoothed by the wash that carried it toward the distant and dry Gila River.

The desert returns to the sea, and the sea comes back. A shell arrived long ago, deep in the desert, and the gravity of the wash is trying to return it. Dunes blow across barren slopes from a dried river in Mexico. Seashells winnow out of the sand a long way from water, not left by waves or storms or some high sea level, but by hands and baskets, people hauling them like currency out of the Sea of Cortez for thousands of years. Bracelets flowed into pre-contact great houses and platform mounds of the north where people who were buried in shell heaps wore them as jewelry. Pueblo sites of dryland farmers and ditch diggers gleamed white with shell bracelets, earbobs, necklaces, pendants, hairpins, while dancers pounded the hardpack of plazas and kiva floors, wildly rattling their ocean-made anklets.

Stand in the middle of the driest place you can think of, wasteland in all directions. The sun is unbroken. The ground is baked, all moisture given up. If you can hold up one object to the orb of the sun, make it a shell, a thing from the sea, a prayer for rain.

I found shells like breadcrumbs. In the beginning, they came to me at random, one among saguaros four hundred miles inland, another, a scallop with drill holes, a friend found in Utah and showed it to me asking what I thought. Kicking around a well-picked archaeological site at the edge of Bears Ears, mined and scattered with broken glass, I found a shell eight hundred miles from any beach, white scroll as long as my finger. It wasn't fossilized, so it didn't end up here through geologic process. Someone, or many someones, carried it.

The material forming a shell is like nothing from the sandstone desert of the Four Corners. Less give than bone, it doesn't splinter or crack like ivory. Its whites are indelible and as bright as snow. A shell forms when a mollusk processes calcium and carbonate ions from seawater, excreting calcium carbonate in crystalline form, making the material actual crystal with a small amount of protein. You can see why it meant something to people whose lives were far more elemental than our own. You'd have to travel far to find something like this.

The shell I found in the Bears Ears was a large *Olivella*, genus of a shell-bearing mollusk that would have come from either southern California or from the Sea of Cortez, mainland Sonora, Mexico. Knowing about the pre-Columbian trade that happened in the Southwest, I'd guess Mexico, not California. That would put its source on beaches looking across toward Baja, beaches I know from when I was a screaming little angel in bumblebee swim shorts, stung by a jellyfish, running for my mom, my blistered red finger outstretched. It's the closest beach to Phoenix where I grew up, a four-hour drive from home in a Volkswagen bug. At a later age, I camped there, bought trinkets from traveling sellers moving up and down the beach, made love, and watched the moon rise over bar-coded ripples on a shallow sea. Dry wind blew through the shade of palapas roofed with dead, bony ocotillo, carrying the smell of tortillas and corvina cooking over a fire.

Over the years, I began noticing more shells on the ground as I traveled in the south, closer to the sea, finding bright flecks, lone shells grayed by fire, one scratched around the edge to make a pattern. In a southern Arizona cave, little beads, tiny *Olivellas*, same genus but different Sea of Cortez species, are in the dirt, as if a slim necklace had broken and they went everywhere. You push them around your palm with a finger, feeling whorls polished by whoever wore these last. Rolled beads of dough, little white pins, you set them back on the ground where they came from, and swish dust across them because the story is not about themselves, but about the cave and where it lies on the land, a place to stop and keep water, a place to sleep out of the wind and drop a small piece of jewelry.

Shell trade was big before Columbus and the seething, unthinkable centuries he kicked off. Before that, shells were ornamentation and industry. Archaeological sites turn up workrooms, entire blocks of pueblos or great houses given to shell craftwork before the Spanish caught wind of this side of the world. These shells flowed with turquoise heading south and live, tropical macaws coming north, a heartbeat rhythm of movement and commerce that thrummed from one desert river to the next.

The Adair Bay, where I ran screaming as a kid, is the nearest big source to Arizona and most of the Southwest. Goods from those beaches left through the blistered Pinacate in northwest Sonora, a volcanic region with pale sands and hard black rock where shell petroglyphs can be found around rainwater tinajas. The trade route beelines north through the long ranges and valleys of Cabeza Prieta where I once counted water holes on a wildlife refuge and its nearby bombing range, where I would find shells in caves and sprinkled on the bajada. These were discarded overburdens from baskets, or mollusks the traders collected to eat, carrying them along the way. Prehistoric processing stations could be reached within two or three days of the beach. Desert communities with plazas and ball courts were weigh stations, ground on which to spread a basket load of shell, sorting through a haul, bartering, trading. The town of Gila Bend and Casa Grande, the city of Tempe and its outliers, Phoenix, Scottsdale, Chandler, Goodyear, are all shell-processing ports, snake towns and platform mounds.

Shells sourced from farther south along the Mexican mainland, around the rich beaches of Bahía Kino, came up through the Sierra Madre, stopping in the ancient desert city of Paquimé where Native craftspeople and laborers worked in dusty chambers, sanding, flaking, and drilling shells by the millions, inlaying some with turquoise and jet before sending them north in bundles and baskets around what is now Nogales or Douglas, Arizona. This is where people now scramble beneath walls, through tunnels, underground railroads, or throw ladders up against a barrier and swiftly get over. Within sight are floodlights at the official border crossing where several million people pass back and forth every year.

I used to travel the border. In the driest parts, people came up from the south and died. I knew that much. I'd see walkers, several shimmering forms miles away, appearing like ghosts and then gone. This is Camino del Diablo, the Devil's Highway. Mass deaths are found year after year, parties succumbed to thirst and heat, people from jungles on their first northward trek, people with children, hands held, marching ahead, people from Hermosillo, Mexico City, Oaxaca, El Salvador, some returnees making a commute, getting in with the wrong group, hot and terrible days. This is where I once found and measured water holes, where I came on boot tracks in gravel, parties passed through the night or the day before. It is also where I found more and more shell on the ground, discards from traders, people of Piman tongue who would have been equipped for these hard rows of mountains, knowing every tinaja, every last storm. They would have been locals stashing cook bowls and ceramic water ollas for their returns.

In the early aughts, I knew the border as a barbed wire fence tangled up in itself, dragged a couple miles south by a flash flood, hung up with cactus parts and stiff, stringy debris. When I found it, and realized what it was, I was not sure how far I'd gone into Mexico without knowing.

Turn of the last century along the Camino del Diablo, which is not an actual highway, but a chain of barren valleys and rocky outcrops, I saw white-painted pylons placed far apart—must have been a quarter mile from one to the next. I had to get out a compass to figure out which country I was in.

Floodlights have gone up, helicopters chopping through the night, the border militarized. Anymore, I keep my travels and overnights to ten or twenty miles to either side of this political line. I camped with my family seventy miles north into Arizona where a team of ATVs showed up, plowing into a turn around us. I caught a glimpse of lettering, federal officers of some sort, maybe. Armored, well-armed, camouflaged, and saddled with battered water bottles and radio gear, they said we were in a travel zone, a pass-through for illegal activity. I would have said that's why we came, because of the pass-through. We were on a trade route looking for rock art, camping for a weekend with the kids. The headman didn't want to hear anything but how soon we'd be leaving. I asked if they were border patrol. He punched his beast into gear, which I think meant yes, or maybe no. Tires dug into gravelly soils. He called over his shoulder as he picked up speed to consider ourselves warned.

We camped up a little side canyon, a place for a tarp strung in the paloverdes. It was national monument land, public access with trails. Three nights later, after we'd explored rock art panels and broken pottery on this long-used desert route, a truck came down to ours in the dark before dawn. It parked at a gravel wash and figures started south with flashlights, upstream along the broad drainage. This lonely mountain range was good cover, and the drainage we'd been exploring made a convenient north-south axis, an inviting geography connecting with Mexico where shells used to come through. An invisible blaze was set in the earth, followed to this day. The walkers inspected our vehicle briefly to see who we were: a family, young kids, parents, four of us at most, our identity visible at a glance through the window.

We lay alert in our bags on the other side of the wash, kids still asleep, listening as these new arrivals moved intently upstream toward a pass, little concerned with the vehicle as they continued out of earshot. Drugs, humans, little plastic toys, shoe polish—I don't know what they were heading up to get or meet. This is what exchange routes are, passages that never stop flowing. This is the Silk Road of North America, a history of pickpockets and semi-trucks hauling opiates across borders, rivers of guns and manufactured goods, money sent back home, relatives brought over, mass graves of murdered women left in barren places, children in cages, and vacationers stuffing bills into donation jars at Mexican checkpoints. I imagine it was cleaner several centuries ago in Native American history, the sound of shells rattling in bags, lines of traders in sandals and bare feet, burdened caciques, no borderline but plenty of languages and territories. They would have been river people, lowlanders, highlanders, warriors in the north, and defensive cliff dwellers in the canyons. Maybe it wasn't easier back then. There would have been raiders and ambushes, clan loyalties, grudges, trade agreements, embargos. Human resources have never been simple.

By dawn we were out of the wash. We told the kids to keep quiet, while sleeping bags, stove, and pans were thrown in the back of our vehicle.

We drove out past the parked truck in early light. A windowless van was parked up higher against saguaros waiting for nothing we knew of. If whatever this was went south, we didn't want to be around. More happens on trade routes than most people know. Active borders are permeable in these corridors where families are being split up, children and infants separated for months or years by the thousands. I see the southern border growing into a Byzantine system of concentration camps, defined by the mass detention of civilians without trial. Detainments go on for years in need of representation, a kind of edifice many were trying to get away from. Ask any shell trader a thousand years ago and they'd tell you that blocking flow in a place like this will be a problem.

A wall might save some, but it'll kill more. One cannot stop what is handed through, or tied to a brick and thrown over, the way you might toss a child to outstretched hands from a burning boat.

One autumn I walked from the desert to the sea, north to south, because trade routes never go one direction alone. I returned to Adair Bay, my first beach with its coarse gravels, bone and shell under soft toddler feet running across sun-crisped feathers and blobs of washed-up jellyfish. Walking back to these beaches some forty years later, I was with two other dads backpacking across a fantastic wasteland of Mexican dunes. I thought of our trek as a ceremony, dancing from desert to sea, several days of dunes and cracked hardpans depositing us at the Sea of Cortez and its shallow, turquoise waters.

We slept on beaches with driftwood fires, ate crabs and small fish, and continued south for another couple of days toward the gleaming circus of Puerto Peñasco. Along the way, I picked up shells; it's not a pilgrimage unless you bring something back. I walked with my thumb rubbing their pearly wells. Most I dropped back to the beach or tossed into the surf like skipping stones. Some I kept. It felt rich, as if we were swimming in shells.

A taqueria stood on a rock point a couple miles across a bay emptied by low tide. Beer and tacos for breakfast we decided, shortcutting the bay, walking straight across on packed wet sand, ripple marks nested with periwinkle shells and fragments of urchins, but the water filled in fast, sole deep, then ankle deep. The last half mile we ran and I imagine we looked like a trio of messiahs boot deep and a mile out to sea, our packs banging against us. We crashed breathless on the other side, dumped our gear on the ground, and watched as the bay filled behind us, pangas with outboard engines crossing where we'd walked and then ran. An American couple, retirement age, strolled by. When the woman glanced at us, the man muttered, Don't make eye contact.

We entered town beered and fed. Passing the Cholla Bay police station, its front door open, we waved at the officer at his desk, who promptly emerged from under the veranda and called us over, frowning at whatever he thought we were. Another officer was brought in, and a third, going through our packs. They found in mine too many shells, some stuffed in zippered pockets, some in bags which they lifted and inspected as if something were hidden inside. Gifts, I said. For friends. This was legal, no?

They asked repeatedly what, really, we were doing. We told them, laughing, that we were crazy, and they didn't believe us at first. Nobody walks in from that gaping, fawn-colored maw. We weren't far from Highway 2, which parallels the border, and a lot happens between here and there, airplane traffic, torn-up runways, and coyotes that walk on two legs. But we had nothing, not a trace of illegal substance, not even an empty tequila bottle. Walking in the desert, our teeth had been needled by sand and we were as clean as we'd ever be, salty and run-down, but polished. The police conceded that we were telling the truth, that we were crazy. They let us go.

We walked back into the same street from a couple hours earlier, sun higher, traffic moving.

A construction flatbed picked us up, heading away from the sea, passing toward the next big town, where the next morning we paid for tickets and boarded a van packed with Mexican nationals, workers heading north with green cards and papers, the morning commute. At the border, US Customs peered through the open van door, seeing Mexicans who looked like riders on a city bus. They also saw the three of us, scruffy *Norté Americanos* of unclear origin or purpose. They had us all get off.

The Mexicans went through with paperwork stamped, ten-minute delay on what was already a busy day. The three of us were held back with a few questions: you came from where, you were doing what, tell me again . . . Our ride left and we took up a wooden bench against a wall, watching the dissection of our packs. One of us had bought a painted jar in town, another had an ashtray or maybe a leathery, taxidermied frog wearing a little sombrero. My bags of shells were laid out on the counter. Ridged and whorled, they must have felt like soap under the quick, gloved touch of a customs agent.

If shells record time, their unstable carbon isotopes decaying like a clock, what else do these hard, crystalline forms remember? Would they tell the story of this stop, one of many in their lives? If you cupped them to your ear, through the seashore hiss you might detect long days of our steps crunching on the beach, and the voices of officials, and the sliding open of a van door. They might remember our fingers grazing through countless centuries, dusty markets with baskets and bags poured on the ground, voices exchanging, artisans scraping and polishing, inlaying small, precious stones.

How much detail these dwindling isotopes give up is hard to know. What about the white-painted cinder block color of this room? Or the growing warzone of the border around us? So much is available to the senses, the smell of smoke from trash fires and exhaust from vehicles moving forward, stopping, moving forward. The other senses, what you know about a place, could curl up in these shells. When you put your ear to it, you'd hear transport trucks loaded with toys, blankets, TVs, guns, and people hidden in containers, breathing slowly in hot, cramped blackness. This, not my hands, is what I wanted the shells to remember. In all this flow, my friends and I were nothing but travelers waiting to get through, pedestrian traders sitting on a bench feeling our bones.

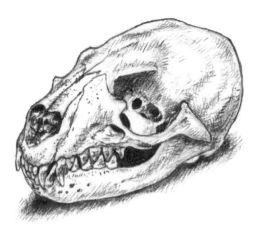

BONE

In the end, only bone remains. Nothing in the desert escapes this brittle reduction.

The hardest, most well-made parts wash up and roll back on an arid beach. Walking to the sea from the desert, you see life reduced to a crystalline line against the water, the last hard pieces of whatever once lived, pelicans, seals, porpoises, whales. The sea hurls life at you, not whole skeletons but fragments, one at a time, slipped into the shallow, pearling surf. Everything here is bone, why desert coasts are called skeleton coasts, easy to run aground. A small boat was wrecked on the long Sea of Cortez tide, washed up and stranded in water not deep enough to float. Its deck had been peeled open, cabin scavenged for parts.

Come inland a short ways, out of earshot of the waves, and find bones: a seal unfolded, having aimed inland as if it were leaving water for good. A crab stands exactly where it had died too far from the sea, its carapace hollow and white from the sun where it had been crossing between soaring cactus, lifted off the ground by the tips of six legs, claws held forward as if still feeling the way.

An unseasonably heavy and unrelenting rain arrived on the mainland coast of Mexico. It lasted longer than one would expect, a few days without pause, a dream in this dry place. In Navajo, this is known as female rain, long, steady, and wetting the deeper roots. In this new moisture, the tall, columnar cactuses turned a dark, wet green. Their accordion skins slowly unfolded, fatter day by day. Clear drips of rain formed at the tip of every spine. I stood with my mouth open drinking from the sky.

Rain is the opposite of bone. It is the start, the earliest tincture of any living thing.

Bone is the end, the last shadow, crystal stone of shell, calcium carapace, marrowed femur or knuckle, life made mineral and left behind. In the rain, I picked up swirls and cones of the stuff, pocketing them to head back to the tent and show my traveling companion, a woman I guided with, a sweetheart from the California coast. This was our off season and we'd gone south toward Bahía

Kino, four hundred miles from the border, the southernmost reach of the Sonoran Desert. We'd hired a panga to motor us up the coast and drop us off with backpacks, and we'd hike back to our starting place in Kino.

For a couple weeks already, we'd been traveling this cactus-lined coast. I'd sketched our finds along the way—owl-killed rodent jaws at the bottom of an ironwood perch, pages of crab claws. This was my bone journal. I found the land decorated with anything unbreakable, the smallest pieces being the most cantankerous: swirled coins of snail opercula, ear bones of birds, little white drums of cochlea.

Stormy days we spent mostly zipped into our shelter. She read Proulx's *Shipping News* out loud, pages turning to sea waves and the wind-swept howl of rain. I darted to the beach to scavenge another round of objects, jaws and spines of sea animals, a lobster carapace curled up. Some she sent back out the tent door, saying get that smelly piece of crap out of here. If they'd rolled long enough in the wrack of this desert-and-sea reunion, the remains tended to smell less putrid, like stone, no more soft tissues to rot. Geometric perfections are what tended to survive, not necessarily the hardest of materials, but architectural particulars. The inside curl of a shell, steeples and spirals, the symmetry of crab breastplates.

The desert is made of remainders. What is soft blows away. You get down to infrastructure, the hinges of fault lines and slender, sweet canyons. This is what dryness offers. Without woods, brambles, or seas of grass, the land chafes to its physical essence, and everything living reduces with it. Friends of mine found in the southern Utah desert a complete human skeleton in a shallow alcove. It was laid out straight and wearied by dust, the person dead and buried, or half-buried, centuries ago. The fallen rib cage had filled with broken rocks spalled off the low, sheltering ceiling. Hips stood up from the dust. The orb of the skull looked like a ceramic vessel. Whomever this person was—daily habits, spiritual beliefs, preference of shade or sunlight—had been diminished to a vault of collagen and calcium. The find wasn't reported to authorities. It was from long enough ago it should stay put, no sense stirring up the dust. The skeleton became part of our landscape, a navigational point, a conversation with a dead person. We didn't spread word about it and eventually we drifted away, exploring other parts of the desert. The bones stayed. I imagine they are still in place, undiscovered, given back to what they do best, drying, splintering, as if begging for rain.

When the storm broke and arroyos stopped running, we packed gear onto our backs and walked south toward Kino, days away past cliff and rock shorelines and gentle plains with waves washing like glass onto the desert. The sea produced its currency. We stopped and shared the skull of a sea lion, shaped like a wolf's or a dog's, and passed back and forth a sea urchin bleached pink and knobbed with rhythmic, artful ossicles. Grinding along this high tide line, I had a sense of why the Tohono O'odham people from both sides of the border send pilgrimages to the sea. Arriving here is a prayer to rain, letting the monsoons rise, the mountains darken, the deserts green. Evidence of every living thing emerges as if summoned.

Rain I welcome, but I like the dry, too. It is a desert after all, a devotion to sun-brittle wood and water holes crisp as parchment. You don't want too much rain. There are old stories about that from desert people, warnings against what you pray for. Tlaloc, an ancient American water god, leaves this place dry on purpose. His imagery appears on rock art across the Southwest, a goggle-eyed figure whose visits are rare and celebrated. He oversees storms and rain. Where he holds back, he reveals the world for what it is. There is no greater worshipper of water than thirst.

To be in the desert is to see under the vellum. Beneath are struts, strands, lines, and cracks. What holds it all together and takes it all apart.

This is where the reason lies. It's not everybody's desired place, too severe, too broken or smooth, hard on the skin, hot on the eyes. You chip and bleed. You find what you are made of.

Pick a bone off the ground. Turn it in your hand, hoping that we all could wear into something as beautiful as a bird wing or the shoulder of a seal. No flesh, no flashy tail, no thought-out panache, this is the hard seed, the last possible breath of something once alive. Pick it up and hold it against a journal page. Read its shadow on paper, the bone and the story it tells.

ABOUT THE AUTHOR

Craig Childs has published more than a dozen books of wilderness and science. He is a contributing editor at *Adventure Journal Quarterly* and his writing has appeared in *The Atlantic, The New York Times, Los Angeles Times, Men's Journal, Orion,* and *High Country News.* He lives outside of Norwood, Colorado.

ABOUT THE COVER

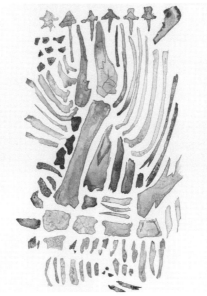

Claire Taylor's painting "Bones of an Unknown Beast" appears on the cover of *Virga & Bone*. The painting depicts bones Claire encountered in the Red Butte Creek Research Natural Area while performing research for a series of wildlife paintings. "Sitting in the canyon arranging the bones for this composition felt as though I was physically handling and sorting through my fears—fear of animals larger than myself and fear of animal death. Creating the painting felt as though it were a collaboration with this unknown fallen beast," Claire states.

Find her work at www.clairetaylor.art.

TORREY HOUSE PRESS

Voices for the Land

The economy is a wholly owned subsidiary of the environment, not the other way around.

—Senator Gaylord Nelson, founder of Earth Day

Torrey House Press is an independent nonprofit publisher promoting environmental conservation through literature. We believe that culture is changed through conversation and that lively, contemporary literature is the cutting edge of social change. We strive to identify exceptional writers, nurture their work, and engage the widest possible audience; to publish diverse voices with transformative stories that illuminate important facets of our ever-changing planet; to develop literary resources for the conservation movement, educating and entertaining readers, inspiring action.

Visit www.torreyhouse.org for reading group discussion guides, author interviews, and more.

As a 501(c)(3) nonprofit publisher, our work is made possible by generous donations from readers like you.

This book was made possible by generous gifts from Jennifer Speers and Anne Milliken. Torrey House Press is supported by Back of Beyond Books, the King's English Bookshop, Jeff and Heather Adams, the Jeffrey S. and Helen H. Cardon Foundation, Suzanne Bounous, the Grant B. Culley Jr. Foundation, Diana Allison, Jerome Cooney and Laura Storjohann, Robert Aagard and Camille Bailey Aagard, Heidi Dexter and David Gens, Kirtly Parker Jones, the Utah Division of Arts & Museums, and Salt Lake County Zoo, Arts & Parks. Our thanks to individual donors, subscribers, and the Torrey House Press board of directors for their valued support.

Join the Torrey House Press family and give today at www.torreyhouse.org/give.